SS-Obersturmbannführer OTTO WEIDINGER

Also by Mark Yerger

WAFFEN-SS COMMANDERS (two volumes)

RIDING EAST: THE SS CAVALRY BRIGADE IN POLAND AND RUSSIA 1939-1942

SS-STURMBANNFÜHRER ERNST AUGUST KRAG

IMAGES OF THE WAFFEN-SS

ALLGEMEINE-SS

SS-Obersturmbannführer

OTTO WEIDINGER

Knight's Cross with Oakleaves and Swords
SS-Panzer-Grenadier-Regiment 4
"Der Führer"

Mark C. Yerger

Schiffer Military History
Atglen, PA

ACKNOWLEDGMENTS

I must first express my deepest thanks to Frau Anneliese Weidinger for her help in the past decade with additional details of her husband in the post-war years. Her positive comment and approval of the manuscript alone was worth all efforts taken to compile it.

My constant appreciation and more is extended to Frau Ruth Sommers for her friendship, help with documents, correspondence and proof-reading. Without her, many details would not be possible and her enthusiasm for my research is always inspiring.

Ignacio Arrondo is both a friend and prolific SS researcher. My sincere appreciation for his help, comments and suggestions is difficult to describe with mere words. My personal hope is to see him compile a text on his specialty area.

Continuous support and suggestions came from James Lucas and Henry Deemer, both of whom command a language skill I hope some day to emulate. They also provide humor beyond comparison.

I also greatly appreciate the time, support and help of Bob Ruman of "Articles of War" and Jack Hatter of "Volume Control." They both diligently pursued the acquisition of a variety of my needed texts so that concentration continues on research itself.

John Moore has provided many years of friendship and help. A dedicated SS historian, his influence is very significant. Mark Burkholder and his family provide friendship and enthusiastic interest for all I research. His dedication to historical preservation is exemplary.

George Nipe is a friend and, in my opinion, the best researcher in the area of battles or campaigns of the Waffen-SS in Russia. His cartographic skills are evident in several of my previous books. I eagerly anticipate the coming release of his Kharkov study.

My sister Leslie still expresses supporting enthusiasm for my books, a topic she has no interest in. Few siblings have a closer relationship of trust, friendship and love. Phil Nix is a stellar SS researcher and friend who, for more than a decade, continues to be supportive in every manner possible. Kurt Imhoff is the most prolific writer on the topic of the Waffen-SS. His help and friendship are a privilege and provide constant motivation. Al Brandt, Martin Mansson, Frank DeLaglio and Jess Lukens continuously help with material and assistance whenever possible in all projects undertaken.

My good friend Gerard Stezelberger and his family have provided humor and friendship in both good and bad times. His attention to detail in our mutual area of interest is both exacting and a constant learning experience.

Lastly, Fred and Ralph continue to be my most constant assistants and distractions. They are family. Mankind would be noticeably improved if our species occasionally emulated some characteristics of cats.

Dedication
To Otto

Book design by Robert Biondi.

Library of Congress Catalog Number: 00-100959.

Printed in China.
ISBN: 0-7643-1169-7

We are always looking for people to write books on new and related subjects. If you have an idea for a book, please contact us at the address below.

Published by Schiffer Publishing Ltd.
4880 Lower Valley Road
Atglen, PA 19310
Phone: (610) 593-1777
FAX: (610) 593-2002
E-mail: Schifferbk@aol.com.
Visit our web site at: www.schifferbooks.com
Please write for a free catalog.
This book may be purchased from the publisher.
Please include $3.95 postage.
Try your bookstore first.

In Europe, Schiffer books are distributed by:
Bushwood Books
6 Marksbury Ave.
Kew Gardens
Surrey TW9 4JF
England
Phone: 44 (0)208 392-8585
FAX: 44 (0)208 392-9876
E-mail: Bushwd@aol.com.
Free postage in the UK. Europe: air mail at cost.
Try your bookstore first.

INTRODUCTION

I assume anyone reading this book has an interest in the Waffen-SS and has absorbed other texts on the topic. My interest in this period is historical, being born more than a decade after the conflict I have no emotional or social connection to the period. Personally considering politics and politicians of any period a non-constructive time expenditure for discussion, I have no interest in either. Politics create the wars that soldiers fight while individuals have opinions arrived at by their own means. Mine are based on the assimilation of data with a resulting conclusion based on objective logic.

War is obviously a ludicrous and destructive undertaking, as any soldier will affirm. In all conflicts, good, bad and average individuals participate among all adversaries. Military men fight for their country and make sacrifices, an admirable characteristic regardless of period or country. In many cases it is the most intense interval of their lifetime.

As a researcher and historian, little can compare to having personal contact with the persons being studied. Only a generation has the opportunity to glean first-hand experiences and information, then interpret individuals based on actually knowing them. That ability has been a privilege and motivation for a lifetime interest in my field of study. I have never tired of learning and understanding.

As a biographical researcher I select topics for specific reasons. Logically, I am much more motivated to research admirable persons possessing positive characteristics. This biography encompasses the career of the man I have come to admire most in my own brief lifetime. This involves respect for the man while examining his entire life, not just his accomplishments as a soldier. If I have managed to make any significant contribution to the study of the Waffen-SS with the books I have written, it was his influence that supplied the most inspiration and objectivity.

My interest in the Waffen-SS has lasted over two decades. As both friend and mentor, Otto Weidinger assisted in all ways possible with my often obsessive desire to learn. This expanded biography incorporates, to the best of my ability, all new photographic and text details or corrections I have obtained in the decade since his death.

Mark C. Yerger
February 2000

OTTO WEIDINGER

The son of Johann and Josepha Weidinger, Otto Weidinger was born in Würzburg on May 27, 1914. As the son of a postal official he spent his childhood in Würzburg and attended Volksschule from 1920 to 1924. His secondary education (Neues Gymnasium) began in 1924 and Weidinger passed his requisite tests for higher education (Abitur) on March 22, 1934. As a student, he especially enjoyed History and German. He also enjoyed and did well in all sports activities made available. Possessing an excellent singing voice, Weidinger enjoyed the opera, when able to attend, and sang in his church choir. Having lost his father in 1923, his social activities revolved around his church group. In later years, he fondly remembered the group's numerous walking and hiking tours and singing.

On July 1, 1933, he joined the Allgemeine-SS as a part-time probationary candidate with the 1./I./56.SS-Standarte, having joined the NSDAP two months earlier. Led by SS-Standartenführer Emil Popp, then SS-Hauptsturmführer Helmut Schulz, the Standarte was located in Würzburg where Weidinger undertook his initial training and served there until April 15, 1934. Transferred to the Wachsturmbann Dachau for further training with its 3rd platoon, he became an SS-Mann on November 24, 1934, holding SS number 114 921. Following his completed training he became an SS-Sturmmann on March 20, 1935. Weidinger qualified for both the Reichs and SA Sports Badges in Bronze during this early training.

Recognized by his superiors as a potential officer, Weidinger was recommended to attend the new SS-Führerschule (Leaders School) in Braunschweig, housed in the former Army cadet school. The school commander, SS-Standartenführer Paul Hausser, would be his most influential tutor and Weidinger would later serve directly with him during the war years.[1] That first Braunschweig class of 1935-1936 included many of the most famous Waffen-SS officers of the war years.[2] Among them were eventual "Leibstandarte" regimental commander and Swords to the Knight's Cross holder Joachim Peiper as well as Franz Augsberger, the first cadet to graduate from that class who attained General officer rank.[3]

Weidinger arrived at the Braunschweig facility during mid-April 1935, in preparation for initial training and indoctrination the following week. All cadets first had the rank of Führeranwärter (officer candidate). When classes formally began at the start of May, cadets were designated as SS-Junker (cadet or officer candidate).[4] After an interval of instruction, Weidinger was promoted to SS-Standartenjunker (intermediate officer cadet) on November 9, 1935.

Following completion of the curriculum at Braunschweig, Weidinger and his fellow cadets attended a Zugführerlehrgang (platoon leaders course) given by SS-Obersturmbannführer Jürgen Wagner at the Dachau training complex. Assigned with recruits from II./SS1 (2nd battalion of SS Standarte 1),

---

[1] Letter to the author from Herr Weidinger dated July 5, 1985. For Hausser's biography see Yerger, "Waffen-SS Commanders, The Army, Corps and Divisional Leaders of a Legend," Volume 1: Augsberger to Kreutz. Other senior commander biographies within that Volume relative to Otto Weidinger's career are Otto Baum, Wilhelm Bittrich, Lothar Debes, Sepp Dietrich and Fritz Klingenberg. With the exception of Debes, who won the German Cross in Silver, all these men were awarded the Knight's Cross. Baum, Bittrich and Hausser won the Swords while Sepp Dietrich was awarded the Diamonds.

[2] Braunschweig was the second officer school established. The first facility was in Bad Tölz and had its initial class in 1934 under school commander Paul Lettow.

[3] See the 1936 SS "Dienstalterliste" for a listing of the 1935/1936 class graduates. Included among them are many of the most famous and highly decorated war-time commanders and staff officers.

[4] "SS-Stammrollen."

Weidinger undertook the course from February 10 to March 30, 1936, and was promoted to SS-Standartenoberjunker (graduate cadet) effective on February 25, 1936. During that time, his initial posting was determined and he went to the 3rd Battalion of SS Standarte 1 as a Zugführer (platoon leader) with the 9.Kompanie (9th Company), the day after completing the platoon leaders course. On April 20, 1936, Weidinger was commissioned as an SS-Untersturmführer and received his officer's sword. The separate battalions first formed for the SS-Verfügungstruppe (SS Special Purpose Troops) formally combined with a staff at the start of July under the command of newly promoted regimental commander, Felix Steiner, to form what became SS-Regiment "Deutschland."[5] Steiner's influence as regimental leader was pivotal for Weidinger as a field officer while he was posted to the 9th Company. His mobile tactics would be implemented during Weidinger's early small-unit commands.

During early July of 1936, a new 3rd Battalion was formed and Weidinger's unit was soon redesignated as the 4th Battalion.[6] As such, his company was renumbered the 16th under battalion commander SS-Obersturmbannführer Willi Schinke.[7]

From the 3rd to the 29th of May 1937, Weidinger attended an engineer platoon leaders course at the SS/VT Pioniersturmbann (Engineer Battalion) base located in Dresden. At the 1937 tournaments in Nuremberg, he placed well with his pack march team. Returning to his "Deutschland" assignment, he was recommended for promotion by Walter Krüger on August 24, 1938, following participation of the unit in the annexation of Austria into the Reich. Krüger took command of the battalion of November 1, 1937. Later, on March 2, 1939, Weidinger was formally awarded the medal for partaking in the events incorporating Austria into the Reich.

During the summer of 1938, Weidinger again left his unit to act as an instructor. He joined Franz Knebel and Hans Weiss as one of the platoon leaders of an NCO Battle School Course led by SS-Hauptsturmführer Willy Fortenbacher near Berchtesgaden.[8] At the completion of the course, Weidinger returned to his unit and on September 11, 1938, was promoted to SS-Obersturmführer. For taking part in the occupation of the Sudetenland, Weidinger was awarded the 1 October 1938 medal on the 27th of that month.

In order to gain experience with an operational Army unit, Weidinger transferred to Jäger (Infantry) Regiment 14 in Weingarten as an officer with the 1st Company from September 24, 1938, until the end of that year. During that time he wore an Army officer uniform with Oberleutnant rank insignia instead of his normal SS attire and the regiment served as a subordinate replacement component of the 5th Military District.

January, 1939, found Weidinger on leave, following which he returned to an SS/VT unit. On the first of February he returned to his previous unit which had become the SS-Kradschützen Bataillon II. Weidinger was assigned as battalion adjutant for this unit being led by SS-Sturmbannführer Udo von Wangenheim. The battalion was a component of SS-Regiment z.b.V. (SS Regiment for Special Deployment) based in Ellwangen under the command of Walter Krüger.[9] Weidinger retained his adjutant post until the unit was dissolved during the summer of 1939.

In June of 1939 the last units were created that would later be components of the initial SS division. During that month, the SS Regiment for Special Deployment was dissolved and used as a basis to form three new formations: the Aufklärungsabteilung SS/VT (reconnaissance detachment) and the Fliegerabwehr-Maschinengewehr-Abteilung SS/VT (antiaircraft detachment) from SS-Motorcycle Battalion II. SS-Motorcycle Battalion I became the SS/VT Panzer-Abwehr Abteilung (anti-tank detachment). Weidinger became the Adjutant of the resulting reconnaissance detachment created from portions of the SS Motorcycle Battalion II that was structured as were similar Army units. Shortly after the unit was formed a new detachment commander was assigned. SS-Sturmbann-

[5] For Steiner's biography see Yerger, "Waffen-SS Commanders, The Army, Corps and Divisional Leaders of a Legend," Volume 2: Krüger to Zimmermann. Other senior commander biographies within that Volume relative to Otto Weidinger's career are Walter Krüger, Heinz Lammerding, Rudolf Lehmann, Hans Mühlenkamp, Sylvester Stadler and Christian Tychsen. All won the Knight's Cross with Oakleaves, Krüger, Stadler and Steiner winning the Swords.

[6] The new SS/VT Standarte (SS 3) was formed in the spring of 1936 but held that title for only a few weeks due to Army objections. The 1st battalion (I./SS 3) was the former III./Deutschland (Ellwangen) and a new 2nd battalion (II./SS 3) was formed in Nuremberg. The I./SS 3 became IV./Deutschland and II./SS 3 became SS-Sturmbann "N" (Nuremberg). "Deutschland" later reduced to the normal three battalion composition of an infantry regiment with four companies per battalion and support units when IV./Deutschland was detached to become part of the SS Regiment for Special Deployment. In March 1938, a new 3rd Regiment of the SS/VT was formed and that became Regiment "Der Führer."

[7] Schinke was killed on July 1, 1941, while commanding the II./SS-Infanterie-Regiment 7.

[8] Knebel served briefly as 1a for the 15.Waffen-Grenadier-Division as an SS-Sturmbannführer before ending the war posted with the SS Officer School in Klagenfurt.

[9] The unit contained SS-Kradschützen Bataillon I and II, the former SS-Bataillon "N" and IV./Deutschland. It was stationed in Ellwangen and Dachau.

führer Dr. Ing. Wilhelm Brandt, the developer of camouflage clothing, assumed command after von Wangenheim transferred to the Luftwaffe.[10] Brandt led the unit in the Polish campaign as part of Panzer Division "Kempf."[11] During this first action the unit was structured as follows:

Stab (Staff)
1.Kradschützen-Kompanie (1st Motorcycle Company)
2.Kradschützen-Kompanie (2nd Motorcycle Company)
Panzerspäh-Zug (Armored Car Platoon)
Panzerabwehr-Zug (Anti-Tank Platoon)

For his performance as reconnaissance detachment adjutant in Poland, Weidinger was awarded the Iron Cross II class on November 15, 1939. During October 1939, the various SS/VT units to be used in the establishment of the premiere SS division were gathered in the Pilsen area under SS-Brigadeführer Paul Hausser.[12] Weidinger remained Adjutant of the Aufklärungsabteilung until November 1, 1939, when he took command of the Panzerspäh-Zug (armored car platoon) and Brandt retained reconnaissance unit command in the new SS-V.T. Division (mot). To assist in his new command, Weidinger attended a Kompanieführer-Lehrgang (Company Commanders Course) during January 1940 in Kitzingen near his home town of Würzburg. Following completion of this course for company level leaders under SS-Sturmbannführer Heinrich Wewerinke, Weidinger returned to his unit.

During early 1940, the platoon that Weidinger commanded was incorporated into the reforming 1st Company and he became commander of the resulting 1.Panzerspäh-Kompanie (armored car company).[13] His command now consisted of three Züge (platoons) of armored cars, one each of light, medium, and heavy (eight-wheeled) armored vehicles. On July 1, 1940, Weidinger was promoted to SS-Hauptsturmführer from a recommendation submitted by his commander. Wilhelm Brandt evaluated Weidinger as follows on September 16, 1940:

> *"SS-Hauptsturmführer Weidinger is a graduate of both high school and the SS officer academy. He possesses an open and honest character. He is a man who unites intelligence, attitude, sporting skills and educational abilities in a special manner. He has served in front line units for more than four years. First a platoon leader, he became an adjutant in mid-1939 and then commanded an armored car company. In all these positions he proved to be excellent.*
>
> *Being well-educated, he possesses tactfulness and good military judgment making him an ideally cooperative leader. His abilities and skill far exceed that required for leading a company. Weidinger fills his assignments to the utmost and is suitable to eventually became a detachment or battalion commander. He seems to be especially suited to serve in the General Staff."*[14]

On July 25, 1940, Weidinger received the Iron Cross 1st class for his performance during the Western campaign. That same day, he married Anneliese Völter during this period when the division was posted to security duties in the Netherlands that lasted until mid-December. Following the recommendations of reconnaissance detachment commander Brandt, Weidinger was selected by commander Paul Hausser to serve on the Divisional Staff. Transferring to the Staff on September 1, 1940, Weidinger undertook the position of 3.Generalstabsoffizier (Intelligence Officer or Ic). In his new staff position Weidinger gained further experience through direct contact with the Divisional commander. As Ic he was assigned an Ordnance

[10] Brandt was killed in Russia as an SS-Obersturmbannführer in command of SS-Infanterie-Regiment 11 on July 13, 1941.

[11] For the actions of the SS/VT units attached to Panzer Division "Kempf," see Weidinger, "Division Das Reich," Volume 1. After the Polish campaign, Werner Kempf led the 6.Panzer Division and in January, 1941, took leadership of the 38th Panzer Corps. During the 1942 Russian campaign he led an Armeeabteilung named for himself. His last field command was the 8th Army and he became Senior Military Commander "Ostland" in May 1944. Awarded the Knight's Cross (June 3, 1940) with Oakleaves (August 10, 1942), he was promoted to General der Panzertruppe on April 1, 1941.

[12] The division had title changes throughout its history as follows: SS-V.T.-Division (mot) (October 10, 1939 to April 1, 1940), SS-V.-Division (April 1, 1940 to November 30, 1940), SS-Division "Deutschland" (December 1, 1940 to January 27, 1941), SS-Division "Reich" (January 28, 1941 to May 1942), SS-Division "Das Reich" (May 1942 to November 9, 1942), SS-Panzer-Grenadier-Division "Das Reich" (November 9, 1942 to January 1944) and the 2.SS-Panzer-Division "Das Reich" (January 1944 to May 1945). The name "Deutschland" was changed to avoid confusion with the regiment of the same name. The unit was a Panzer Division in composition after its Panzer Regiment was established in October 1942. Yerger, Mark C.: "Knights of Steel, The Structure, Development and Personalities of the 2.SS-Panzer-Division "Das Reich," Volume 1.

[13] The reconnaissance detachment underwent an almost continuous change of structure during its existence. A third motorcycle company was added in April, 1940, though initially it had no vehicles. That 3.Kompanie was moved to the separate Motorcycle Battalion the following February. By the invasion of Russia the unit had one each of anti-tank, armored car and motorcycle companies. In the spring of 1943 it absorbed the dissolved motorcycle battalion, that had become the I./Langemarck in 1942, and at the end of the war contained five companies led by Oakleaves winner Ernst August Krag. Herr Weidinger's diary notes and award documents confirm his command of the Reconnaissance Detachment's 1st Company with numerous photos of him as Panzerspäh Kompanie Chef among vehicles of the unit.

[14] SS-V. Aufklärungsabteilung, "Beurteilung," dated September 16, 1940.

Officer (03) to assist in his duties, SS-Untersturmführer Erwin Mix.[15]

On November 1, 1940, Weidinger became the Divisional Adjutant for Officers (IIa) and held this position for some time as well as Divisional Adjutant for NCOs and enlisted men (IIb). He remained the Divisional Adjutant during the Yugoslavian campaign and the following operational preparations for the Russian offensive while "Reich" assembled in Austria.

The opening battles of June 1941, as well as the fast-paced combats of the Western campaigns, had amply demonstrated that high-speed units were effective casualty-savers. Consequently, the Division had formed a Kradschützen Bataillon (motorcycle battalion) in mid-February 1941.[16] The Russian campaign was costly, especially among the leading units. Soon after the invasion of Russia, initial motorcycle battalion commander August Zehender was wounded on June 29, 1941, and famed Knight's Cross holder Fritz Klingenberg assumed command.

On July 13, 1941, Weidinger replaced SS-Obersturmführer Joachim Wüstenberg as commander of the 5th (schwere/heavy) Company of the Motorcycle Battalion.[17] Slightly more than two weeks later the commander of the unit's 3rd Company, SS-Hauptsturmführer Christian Tychsen, was wounded. Weidinger took over command of this unit on 30 July 1941. His leadership and bravery were instantly recognized.

> *"On July 30, 1941, the enemy attacked the positions held by the 3rd Company of the Motorcycle Battalion "Das Reich" in the Jelnya area with an Infantry Division and strong artillery support. In the 14.2 kilometer-wide section of the Company, all positions were bitterly defended by all marksmen, drivers, and supply handlers. The enemy, who had been able to break through, were destroyed in close combat. In the crisis of this breakthrough, the commander was wounded and SS-Hauptsturmführer Weidinger took over leadership of the unit.*
>
> *Although Weidinger was absolutely new to the Company, immediately after arrival he put himself in charge of a quickly-organized assault detachment in order to overcome the enemy troops that had been able to reach the trenches in a counter-attack. In an uninterrupted hard battle which lasted for 24 hours, SS-Hauptsturmführer Weidinger fought from trench-to-trench until the whole system of trenches was solidly in our hands.*
>
> *The enemy attacked these positions again and again, which, at that time, reached furthest to the east, with a tremendous expenditure of people and material. The enemy left behind within the sector of the Company 480 dead and a great number of wounded. The only machine gun of the assault detachment, which was led by SS-Hauptsturmführer Weidinger, fired 21,000 rounds in this battle alone."*[18]

Weidinger remained with this Company during the early months of the first Russian campaign, gaining a reputation for calmness and bravery in extreme situations.

> *"On September 3, 1941, north of Awdejewka, the SS-Motorcycle Battalion was ready to start the attack as the spearhead for "Reich" the following day. In the morning the commander got in touch with the section of the 10th Infantry Division (motorized) that was located in Awdejewka. They were defending the area, under the leadership of the Ib, with reinforcements and 1st Infantry Company. At this time the Russians attacked with one Infantry Battalion and three tanks. Most of the forces put into action ran away in full flight. The command of the whole section of Awdejewka was then transferred to SS-Hauptsturmführer Weidinger. He quickly divided the sections of 10th Infantry Division among his own troops. With iron energy and partly by fighting hardest himself, he created order in this confused sector. He led the counterattack in a dashing defense. It was due to his initiative and his cold blooded dash that the old positions could be taken back and the village held. Late in the afternoon, the Russians attacked in regimental strength. Portions of*

[15] Mix ended the war as an SS-Sturmbannführer serving on the staff of the II.SS-Panzer-Korps as Ic (Intelligence Officer) after holding the same post with the 10.SS-Panzer-Division "Frundsberg."

[16] "Aufstellung eines Kradsch. Btl. Bei SS-Div. "Reich," dated February 20, 1941, and issued by the SS-Führungshauptamt. The battalion consisted of three motorcycle companies, a machine gun company and a heavy company with three platoons (engineer, light infantry gun and anti-tank). The companies were drawn from existing units of the Reconnaissance Detachment, "Deutschland," "Der Führer," and SS-Infanterie Regiment 11. The battalion became a component of Regiment "Langemarck" in 1942 and the following year was dissolved to be used for rebuilding the Reconnaissance Detachment. For the detailed history of the Kradschützen Bataillon, see Yerger, Mark C.: "Knights of Steel, The Structure, Development and Personalities of the 2.SS-Panzer-Division "Das Reich," Volume 2, pages 12-73.

[17] Soon after returning to his company command, Wüstenberg was wounded. He died at the SS hospital in Braunschweig on November 8, 1941.

[18] "Vorschlagliste Nr. 93 für die Verleihung des Deutschen Kreuzes in Gold" dated November 13, 1943, and signed by Walter Krüger.

Weidinger's troops began to pull back but the commander forced them back to the front-line area. With his example in battle, he prevented the enemy from breaking through our positions. Any breach by the enemy would have endangered the divisional attack ordered for the next day.

On September 4, 1941, at 4:30, the reinforced SS-Motorcycle Battalion "Das Reich" made ready for the attack west of Awdejewka against district Dedy. The 3rd Company, with parts of 10th Infantry division (motorized), was ready for the defense at the eastern border and had the order to follow the Battalion as a reserve unit after the attack got under way. As soon as the Battalion had overrun the anterior positions of the enemy with "HURRAH", parts of the enemy in the lines by Awdejewka also went back. SS-Hauptsturmführer Weidinger used this weakness capably in proper recognition of the situation, crashed with "HURRAH" in front of his Company out of his own positions. They ran over the enemy and conquered, with his Company now fighting at the head of the Battalion, the target which the Battalion was ordered to attack. The Company took 200 prisoners and as booty 30 machine guns and four anti-tank cannons. Although SS-Hauptsturmführer Weidinger was wounded during the attack, he bravely stayed with his unit until the objective of the attack was reached and only then did he allow himself to be taken to the main dressing station."[19]

On September 4, 1941, Weidinger was shot in the lower left leg, a wound that resulted in his being awarded the Wound Badge in Black. After his recovery in the hospital, he returned to front line duty during the second week of October, 1941. On October 15, 1941, Weidinger took command of the 1st Company of the Motorcycle Battalion. He replaced SS-Hauptsturmführer Wilhelm Kment who moved to take command of the Reconnaissance Detachment after Hans Mühlenkamp was wounded.[20] Although this command lasted only a week, Weidinger's leadership was noted with further superlative efforts:

"On October 19, 1941, SS-Hauptsturmführer Weidinger attacked, after the defense positions near Moscow had been breached, with the 1st Company of the Motorcycle-Battalion, the heavily fortified positions at the east crossing of the railway south of Moscow near Josevo. In bitter hand-to-hand combat the Company forced its way through the stubbornly defended positions. When the 3rd section leader was killed in action, Weidinger personally took over leadership of the lead section and stormed the last of the enemy positions. The counterattack which followed immediately and was fortified by tanks, was beaten back by Weidinger in heavy hand-to-hand combat. While doing this, Weidinger was again wounded while personally destroying an enemy tank."[21]

SS-Sturmbannführer Fritz Klingenberg signed the document awarding Weidinger the Infantry Assault Badge in Bronze on October 21, 1941. The following day Weidinger was relieved of his command and ordered back to Germany for reassignment. That same day he and his wife Anneliese became the proud parents of their first daughter, Brigitte.

The losses suffered in Russia, combined with the transfer of prewar officer school instructors, necessitated the use of graduates with combat experience as teachers at the two SS officer schools. Weidinger was assigned to his alma mater, the SS-Junkerschule in Braunschweig, where he reported on November 1, 1941, to school commandant Lothar Debes. His skills and ability as an instructor were acknowledged by the school's commandant in a September, 1942, evaluation.

"SS-Hauptsturmführer Weidinger was ordered to SS-Junkerschule Braunschweig where he is engaged as a tactics instructor. He is a well-balanced, mature personality and his character is without fault. Mentally lively and interested in all military facets, he stimulates his surroundings as good company. He is by nature quiet and rational. A military versatility at the front line and in staff posts, among the latter divisional adjutant, made it possible for him to acquire extensive tactical knowledge. Therefore he

[19] Ibid.

[20] Letter to the author from Herr Weidinger dated September 9, 1985. A graduate of SS officer school Bad Tölz, Kment served as an armored car and motorcycle company commander through his promotion to SS-Hauptsturmführer on September 1, 1940. He returned to Bad Tölz as an instructor before joining the Motorcycle Battalion as commander of the 1.Kompanie. After being wounded in February, 1942, commanding the Reconnaissance Detachment and losing an arm, Kment became the decorations officer for the Waffen-SS, assigned to handle recommendations for the Knight's Cross and German Cross. Kment himself won the German Cross in Gold on January 23, 1942, for actions while assigned to the Motorcycle Battalion of "Reich," being promoted to SS-Sturmbannführer on June 21, 1943, and to SS-Obersturmbannführer on November 9, 1944. He died on November 15, 1984.

[21] "Vorschlagliste Nr. 93 für die Verleihung des Deutschen Kreuzes in Gold" dated November 13, 1943, and signed by Walter Krüger.

is especially suited to his present post and is judged to be very effective in organizing the tactical instructions in an interesting way. On the grounds of his education and tactical abilities, Weidinger would be especially suitable for a career in the General Staff."[22]

Utilizing his field experience, Weidinger taught and led cadets until May, 1943. During his initial instructing assignment he was awarded the War Merit Cross II class on January 31, 1943.[23] For the month of January, 1943, he attended the 5.Abteilungsführerlehrgang für schnelle Truppen (Detachment Leaders Course for Fast Troops) at the Heeres-Abteilungsführerschule (Army Detachment Leaders School) in Paris. Following the completion of this course he returned to Braunschweig. Under school commandant SS-Oberführer Werner Ballauf, who took over for Debes at the start of 1942, Weidinger became commander of Lehrgruppe (Teaching Group) "B" at the start of February 1943.[24] He stayed in command of this unit until given new orders in mid-May, 1943, teaching cadets of the 9th wartime class to undertake officer training who finished training at the end of that month. Weidinger was then again reassigned to "Das Reich." His posting in Germany allowed him precious time with his growing family. His second daughter, Sigrid, was born on May 1, 1943. On May 8, 1943, Braunschweig commandant Ballauf submitted a recommendation that Weidinger be promoted to SS-Sturmbannführer.

Upon arriving at the front and being briefed, Weidinger was given command of the 1st Battalion of Regiment "Deutschland." This was his first combat battalion-level command as the replacement for SS-Obersturmbannführer Fritz Ehrath.[25] His command authority became effective on June 1, 1943, the date of his newly approved promotion to SS-Sturmbannführer. Weidinger led this unit for two months during history's largest armored battle (Kursk) and in the heavy fighting near the Mius river. On August 5, 1943, Weidinger obtained his first tactically independent command when he replaced SS-Sturmbannführer Jakob Fick (who was wounded) as commander of the "Das Reich" Reconnaissance Detachment.[26]

"When the enemy near Ljubotin (southeast of Kharkov) forced its way into the section of the town called Staraja-Ljubotin, SS-Sturmbannführer Weidinger received the order for his unit to clear this section of the enemy and return after completing the assignment. When SS-Sturmbannführer Weidinger drove ahead of his unit to get in touch with the furthermost parts of an artillery position, he recognized that the enemy had broken through our lines at the further to the westerly village of Schpakowka. The enemy was preparing to attack the southern part of Ljubotin in order to capture our own units that were fighting to the north at the Udy.

After further reconnaissance, SS-Sturmbannführer Weidinger confirmed the Russians were marching from Schpakowka towards the south without being stopped. He then immediately decided to go into blocking positions, with his units on the heights near Starja-Ljubotin. That move was in order to stop the enemy who advanced with tanks, and to halt the breakthrough at all costs. Because of his willingness to personally give his best, SS-Sturmbannführer Weidinger was able to bring in the mobile units quickly and to occupy the crucial heights before the Russians got there. The enemy found a defensive front which was still rather weak but became continuously stronger. Only through untiring exemplary effort by the commander, who again and again appeared at the center of the battle and inspired by his example, was it possible for this small group to defy the first enemy attacks. For six days the en-

[22] SS-Junkerschule Braunschweig, Kdo. Az: Ba./o., "Beurteilung," dated September 7, 1942 and signed by Werner Ballauf.

[23] See award document illustration. Though the document shows the formal award date, Herr Weidinger asserts he was given the actual medal during April 1942 at Braunschweig.

[24] Ballauf joined the SS in 1933 as an SS-Sturmbannführer and led the Nachrichtenabteilung (Signals Detachment) SS/VT from September 1935 to the start of July 1936. He then held staff post and command of III./Deutschland until November 1938. From December 1938, to October 1939, he was with "Der Führer" and the follwing month became SS Standortkommandant in Prague until January 1941. During the first half of 1941, Ballauf led the 10.SS-Totenkopf-Standarte and then commanded SS-Infanterie-Regiment 6. Promoted to SS-Oberführer on November 9, 1941, he went to the SS-Führungshauptamt until taking command of Braunschweig in January 1942. Promoted to SS-Brigadeführer on April 20, 1943, he was commandant of Braunschweig until the school was destroyed by an air attack in February 1945. Ballauf spent the remaining months of the war attached to Armeeoberkommando 1.

[25] Ehrath won the Knight's Cross as an SS-Obersturmbannführer in command of Regiment "Germania" on February 23, 1944. As an SS-Sturmbannführer commanding I./Der Führer, he won the German Cross in Gold on January 10, 1943, serving with "Das Reich."

[26] An early member of the SS/VT, Fick initially served with "Deutschland." He then led the Anti-aircraft Detachment and also served as an instructor at the Braunschweig and Bad Tölz SS officer schools. Moving to "Das Reich" in 1942, Fick won the Knight's Cross on April 23, 1943, for his leadership of the Motorcycle Battalion during the Kharkov battles. After commanding the Reconnaissance Detachment of "Das Reich" before moving to the 17.SS-Panzer-Grenadier-Division "Götz von Berlichingen" as regimental commander of SS-Panzer-Grenadier-Regiment 38. Promoted to SS-Standartenführer on January 30, 1945, he survived the war. For details of the actions resulting in his award of the Knight's Cross, see Yerger: "Knights of Steel," Volume 2, pages 49-50.

emy attacked the positions of the unit again and again with the help of strong tank, artillery and mortar fire. He was repeatedly able to break through. Again and again it was SS-Sturmbannführer Weidinger who scraped together a few men and cleaned up the situation with unheard-of brave initiative and dash. Again and again he motivated the melted-down groups of his unit, by his shining example, to the highest of resistance. Only in this way could theses positions be held that long. They were evacuated according to orders on August 28/29."[27]

On August 19, 1943, Weidinger was awarded the Wound Badge in Silver. He had been wounded twice since his award of the grade in black: on July 8th by shell fragments in the chest and on August 12, 1943, by shrapnel in the head and shoulder.

Five days later Weidinger's unit entered combat with components of a Soviet Panzer Brigade. In Weidinger's opinion, the combat was the most severe of all those he encountered in the course of his military service.

"On September 9, 1943 the SS-Reconnaissance Detachment 'Das Reich' was put into action east of Kolomak on the right wing of the Division. In front of this section of the Abteilung more than 100 tanks appeared, of which 80 made ready for a direct attack on the position of the Abteilung. 60 tanks rolled over the unit. Due to the superior and brave leadership which created trust among the men, the unit allowed itself to be run over by the tanks and took up the uneven battle afterwards united with a tank company of the Division. At this section SS-Sturmbannführer Weidinger was always at the head of the troops. Near his battle station at the front of the line 22 enemy tanks (out of 59 total) were disabled."[28]

"Das Reich" continued intensive fighting along the Dnieper river as part of 11th Army Corps with especially severe combats in the vicinity of Poltawa. From the start of its offensive in Russia until mid-September 1943, the Division destroyed 1,400 enemy armored vehicles. By the end of the war "Das Reich" destroyed more than 4,800 enemy vehicles and as such was the most successful German Panzer Division. The Division was also awarded more Knight's Crosses than any other unit of the Waffen-SS.[29]

"In the big loop of the Dnieper river the enemy attacked anew on October 15, 1943, in order to connect the big bridgehead with the little one by Schtschutzinka and by doing so, to be able to cut off our own troops who fought in the corridor between the enemy bridgeheads. By this attack, which was made by two battalions on Chodoroff, a 1,200 meter-wide opening was created because of the flight of members of a 2cm anti-aircraft battery between the Army 266th Infantry Regiment and the Reconnaissance Detachment in which, except for the abandoned machine gun, there was not a single German soldier left. The Russians surged into the opening behind the fleeing Army anti-aircraft members and threatened to turn the flank from the back of the area engaged in a heavy defensive battle. SS-Sturmbannführer Weidinger recognized from his neighboring section the danger which threatened him as well as the two corridor sections. But he had to work hard to hold his own section with his strongly-reduced unit.

He could not spare a single man from his unit. With messengers and drivers of some supply units who were in the area by chance, a total of six men and two machine guns, he himself made a counterattack into the side of the enemy streaming into the breach. By cleverly using his men and with exceptionally brave effort, it was possible for him to slow down the further-advancing enemy. In spite of their support from artillery, through flanking machine gun fire he inflicted considerable losses upon them. Together with later-arriving assault weapons, SS-Sturmbannführer Weidinger was able to iron out the area of the breakthrough. Later, the old positions were again occupied by members of the anti-aircraft unit who were brought back by the assault gun detachment."[30]

Divisional commander Walter Krüger filed a recommendation for Weidinger to be awarded the German Cross in Gold

[27] "Vorschlagliste Nr. 93 für die Verleihung des Deutschen Kreuzes in Gold" dated November 13, 1943, and signed by Walter Krüger.

[28] Ibid.

[29] 73 men of "Das Reich" were awarded the Knight's Cross, with "Wiking" being second with 54. Regiment "Der Führer" alone had 17 and many men were awarded higher grades during later service with other units. "Das Reich" destroyed more enemy armored vehicles than any other formation (over 4800) despite not having an operational tank regiment in combat until 1943.

[30] Ibid.

on October 23, 1943. After approval by higher echelons the decoration was awarded on November 26, 1943. The five pages of testimony ended with:

> *"SS-Sturmbannführer Weidinger shows himself at all engagements of the Division to be an outstanding troop leader. His bravery, together with a cautious dash, is exemplary and well-known within the division. His decoration with the German Cross seems to me particularly indicated."*[31]

Remaining commander of his Detachment, Otto Weidinger engaged in what was, in his opinion, the second most severe combat of his career east of Shitomir during November, 1943. This occurred, it should be noted, with the unit as far less than peak strength as the division had been at an offensive spearhead position for more than six months.

> *"In the heavy defensive battles east of Shitomir, an SS-Reconnaissance Detachment patrol, under the daring leadership of SS-Sturmbannführer Weidinger, proved itself repeatedly in an outstanding performances. On November 22, 1943, the patrol was engaged in a heavy defensive battle in the area around Negrebowka. To the north of the patrol were two enemy Regiments while west of it a strong force of anti-tank weapons blocked off and defended an enemy breakthrough towards the south near Sabelotsche. When the enemy troops breached the positions of the Reconnaissance Detachment in two placed, it was Weidinger who, in personally conducted counterattacks, cleaned up the inroads of the enemy again and again.*
>
> *In the afternoon the enemy was able to gain a wide breakthrough at the neighboring position to the right and continued pushing until the whole Detachment was encircled. Even in this situation Weidinger kept a clear head and ordered a counterattack with his weak reserves.*
>
> *Although to the west a five-kilometer-deep open flank had to be defended, Weidinger pulled out his reserve. In order to halt the break in a counterattack, he fought at night beside parts of the 2nd and 3rd Companies. With 17 men, Weidinger personally threw himself against the enemy forces who had broken through the northern part of Negrebowka, stopped the attack, and pushed the enemy back over the main line in a counterattack that inflicted severe Russian losses. Although Weidinger had orders to avoid stronger enemy resistance, he held his position until armored group 'Stadler' brought relief. Due to his initiative and determination, his personal bravery and superior example, the bridgehead at Negrebowka could be held. This was the basis for the successful attack of the 1.SS-Panzer-Grenadier-Division "Leibstandarte SS Adolf Hitler" and the 2nd Paratroop Division."*[32]

Having fought in continuous exhaustive combat since the February Kharkov battles, the terrible losses of "Das Reich", as well as the other units of Hausser's SS-Panzer-Korps, required a complete refit. Consequently, plans were instituted for reforming as a Panzer Division. Commander Walter Krüger would return to France with the majority of the Division for reforming. However, the situation at the front required that "Das Reich" leave behind a Kampfgruppe (battle group) to be employed in conjunction with the remaining Army units. Formed in mid-December, 1943, Battle Group "Das Reich" contained slightly more than 5,000 men.

The initial commander of Battle Group "Das Reich" was the Division's First Staff Officer or Ia, SS-Obersturmbannführer Peter Sommer.[33] Weidinger remained in Russia with the other designated members of the Battle Group. From the 17th to the 28th of December he commanded a composite Army Replacement Regiment, taking over command from SS-Sturmbannführer Hans Weiss who returned to East Prussia to assist in the rebuilding of the Panzer Regiment's Panther Detachment. Weidinger's command for this period consisted of the Army's Engineer Battalion 87, Armored Reconnaissance Detachment 25, and Armored Engineer Battalion 19.[34]

The commander of the Battle Group's Panzer Grenadier Regiment (Armored Infantry Regiment), SS-Sturmbannführer Hans Bissinger, was appointed the Battle Group Ia and on December 28, 1943, Weidinger took command of the Regiment.[35] His first Waffen-SS Regimental level command consisted of

[31] Ibid.

[32] "Vorschlagliste Nr. 33 für die Verleihung des Ritterkreuzes des Eisernen Kreuzes," dated April 3, 1944, and signed by Heinz Lammerding.

[33] Won the German Cross in Gold on January 10, 1943. For his biography and photos see Yerger, "Knights of Steel," Volume 1, pages 80-81.

[34] These three units were originally components of the 25.Panzer Division and 19.Panzer Division.

[35] Bissinger won the German Cross in Gold on April 24, 1943, for leadership of II./Deutschland and ended the war as an SS-Obersturmbannführer in command of SS Field Replacement Brigade 6.

troops formerly contained in the 1st Battalion of SS-Regiment "Deutschland" and the 2nd Battalion of SS-Regiment "Der Führer." A partial list of the units and commanders of Battle Group "Das Reich" at this time was as follows:

Commander: SS-Obersturmbannführer Peter Sommer
Ia: SS-Sturmbannführer Hans Bissinger
Adjutant: SS-Obersturmführer Ernst Gerwig
Technical Officer: SS-Obersturmführer Dr. Ernst Müller
Armored Infantry Regiment "Das Reich": SS-Sturmbannführer Otto Weidinger
Tank Detachment "Das Reich": SS-Hauptsturmführer Franz Endemann
1st Reconnaissance Company: SS-Hauptsturmführer Heinrich Wulf[36]
1st Engineer Company: SS-Hauptsturmführer Heinrich Schmelzer[37]
Heavy Infantry Company: SS-Obersturmführer Georg Seegerer
Two Assault Gun Companies: SS-Hauptsturmführer Hans-Joachim Mützelfeld[38]

The Battle Group also contained an anti-aircraft contingent, its own support elements, as well as other components assigned to it when available or needed from adjacent SS and Army units.

On December 28, 1943, SS-Oberführer Heinz Lammerding was appointed Battle Group commander. He arrived in early January, 1944, and relieved SS-Obersturmbannführer Peter Sommer who left to become Walter Krüger's Chief of Staff for the VI.SS-Freiwilligen-Armeekorps. Weidinger continued to lead his regiment, as the largest component of the Battle Group, in battles in Ostropol, Lyuba, and Staro-Konstantinov during the first months of 1944. Due to attrition and casualties, the composition and commanders of the Battle Group changed often during the months of its existence.

On January 30, 1944, Heinz Lammerding was selected to command the entire "Das Reich" Division. He would replace Walter Krüger who left to undertake his new corps command. However, Lammerding remained with the Battle Group until March. Portions of "Das Reich" continued reforming in France under the leadership of the senior regimental commander, SS-Standartenführer Sylvester Stadler, who also commanded SS-Regiment "Der Führer." When Lammerding left, Weidinger took command of the remainder of the Battle Group on March 8, 1944. From this date the unit was designated Battle Group "Weidinger."

During Weidinger's tenure as commander, the Battle Group was encircled in the Kamenez-Podolsk pocket along with other units that composed the 1st Panzer Army. These units were held fast by superior Russian forces until relieved by II.SS-Panzerkorps under the command of SS-Obergruppenführer Paul Hausser. Following rescue by units of the Korps, the remaining elements of the Battle Group were placed in reserve in readiness for transfer to France. On April 20, 1944, Weidinger led his men on transport trains back towards Germany and then to Toulouse, France, to join the rest of "Das Reich."

When commander Lammerding had returned to France, he submitted a recommendation for Weidinger to be awarded the Knight's Cross of the Iron Cross. It was approved by Hitler on April 21st for those difficult battles while commanding the Reconnaissance Detachment in 1943. As Weidinger boarded the train for his return to France he was unaware of his award. I inquired of Herr Weidinger when he heard of his decoration and if it was noticed by the public on his return. He replied as follows:

> *"When, after heavy casualties and fighting, we were finally pulled out of the Eastern Front, we moved by rail across Germany to France beginning April 20, 1944. On April 27th our transport train (about 800 men strong) arrived at our destination. At the Toulouse railroad station, march tunes reached us and then the military band of Regiment "Deutschland" came into view, lined up for our welcome. In front stood the Regimental Commander, SS-Obersturmbannführer Günther Wisliceny, who warmly greeted the Battle Group in the name of the Divisional Commander. At that time he congratulated me for the award of the Knight's Cross, of which I was completely unaware. It was awarded to me for the actions at Negrebowka as commander of the Reconnaissance Detachment*

[36] In 1944 commanded the divisional Reconnaissance Detachment and was recommended for the German Cross in Gold for service with the Battle Group.

[37] Won the German Cross in Gold on October 27, 1942, and the Knight's Cross for actions leading his unit of the Battle Group on March 12, 1944. As a company commander leading the 1./Pionier Bataillon "Das Reich," Schmelzer won the Oakleaves on February 28, 1945. For his biography and photos, see Yerger: "Knights of Steel," Volume 2, pages 184-185. He died on April 4, 1985.

[38] Won the German Cross in Gold on November 26, 1943 while commanding the 3./Flak Abteilung "Das Reich." He later became Ia of the II.SS-Panzer-Korps then held the same post with the 20.Waffen-Grenadier-Division der SS as an SS-Obersturmbannführer.

'Das Reich', just at the time our transport train was rolling across Germany.

While the Battle Group marched to the prepared barracks buildings, I drove to the Divisional Headquarters at Montauban to officially report the return of the Battle Group to the Divisional Commander, SS-Brigadeführer Heinz Lammerding.

I was warmly greeted by him and his staff and then decorated by him with the Knight's Cross. A small celebration with my comrades concluded this memorable day for me.

The next morning the entire Battle Group was formed into open square in the court of Toulouse Barracks for a reception by the Divisional Commander. He thanked all the officers, NCOs, and enlisted men for their outstanding performances, which were already appreciated by the awarding of a large number of Iron Cross I class and Iron Cross II class by the 59th Army Corps. He congratulated me as commander of the Battle Group and for the award of the Knight's Cross.

In my short reply I stated that I was wearing the Knight's Cross for the great achievements of the entire Battle Group, which had been impenetrable in attack and defense during the four-month long withdrawal operations from Shitomir to the hard fought-for Hill 347 near Slone. Afterwards the different units of the dissolved Battle Group 'Das Reich' returned to their base units.

During the following leave I continuously received preferred and respectful treatment as a Knight's Cross bearer, from the population. Such as when I found a seat in a fully occupied train and wanted to offer it to a woman with a child, who had boarded the train after me, and absolutely refused to accept it. Only after an energetic talking to could I convince her to do so.

At home, the city of Aalen had prepared a formal reception for me in the city hall, which the Mayor with the town council, the district party representative, the notables of the city, and the commander of the Army Remount School attended. Mayor Schubel congratulated me for this high decoration and stated the city of Aalen was proud of her Knight's Cross bearer. Then the district party representative and the commander of the school, Colonel Angerer, offered their congratulations. My wife received a giant bouquet of flowers and then I signed my name into the Golden Book of the city of Aalen.

After this, my family went with the dignitaries to the hotel 'Crown Olga' for a drink, and there I was presented with an oil painting of the source of the river Kocher as a gift from the city of Aalen.

Also, during the following short leave in Germany, my wife and I were extended special treatment everywhere. For instance, in reserving a hotel room which were very hard to find at the time. At the Zugspitz railroad station I was immediately passed on to the ticket office by a long line of waiting people to obtain my ticket first. Up top in the Zugspitz Hotel, we were guided by the chief receptionist to two reserved seats in the glassed-in veranda with a magnificent view of the mountain panorama. Thus, Germany honored her Knight's Cross bearers in those days."[39]

On April 30, 1944, Weidinger was again decorated, this time with the Bronze Close Combat Clasp. Following his return from leave, Weidinger was given his next assignment.

Upon returning to "Das Reich" Weidinger was posted to SS-Regiment "Der Führer" as head of training under commander SS-Standartenführer Sylvester Stadler. The entire Division was alerted for combat following the Normandy landings and advanced towards that area. During this time Regimental Commander Stadler was promoted to command a full division and left to undertake training for his new assignment. On June 14, 1944, Otto Weidinger became the fourth and last commander of SS-Panzer-Grenadier-Regiment 4 "Der Führer", which was among the strongest and most decorated Waffen-SS Regiments.[40] His battalion commanders were SS-Sturmbannführer Adolf Diekmann (1st battalion), SS-Sturmbannführer Herbert Schulze (2nd battalion) and SS-Hauptsturmführer Heinz Werner (3rd battalion).[41] During the first month of his command, Weidinger fought in the area near Caen and in La-Haye-de-Puits as commander of an independent Battle Group. After heavy fighting near Mortain, the units of "Das Reich" continued the withdrawal towards Germany. The Divi-

[39] Letter to the author from Herr Weidinger dated October 10, 1986. Günther Wisliceny, the last commander of Regiment "Deutschland," won both the Oakleaves and the Swords to the Knight's Cross on the same day as Weidinger, ending the war as an SS-Obersturmbannführer. He died on August 25, 1985.

[40] Georg Keppler, Otto Kumm and Sylvester Stadler were the previous commanders. 17 members of the regiment were awarded the Knight's Cross.

[41] Dieckmann was killed on June 29, 1944. Schulze won the Knight's Cross on December 16, 1943, and commanded the 2nd battalion from July 1943 until wounded in August 1944. He died on February 2, 1992. Werner succeeded Knight's Cross holder Helmut Kämpfe when the latter was murdered in France on June 9, 1944.

sion managed to avoid the encirclement in Falaise which trapped a large number of troops. As the strongest unit outside the pocket, "Das Reich" provided the forces to hold the trap open and provide a corridor of escape for the trapped Army and Waffen-SS units. Weidinger's command, operating as a Battle Group, was assigned this critical mission. For his leadership and ability in helping extract these otherwise doomed units, Weidinger was recommended for the Oakleaves to the Knight's Cross by Heinz Lammerding on November 30, 1944, with the following report:

"On August 19, 1944, SS-Panzer-Grenadier-Regiment 4 'Der Führer' received the order to push forward to the west along the road Trun.-St. Lambert, in order to make contact with the German forces almost encircled in the pocket of Falaise-Argentan and help them disengage.

On August 20th, "Der Führer," with a force of 11 officers, 53 NCOs and 366 enlisted men under the leadership of SS-Sturmbannführer Weidinger, entered towards the area of Champosoult. In an uninterrupted attack the Regiment reached the intersection of the road 1 kilometer northeast of Coudehard at 12am. The Regimental Commander, leading the foremost company, pulled his men along.

By 1pm the enemy pressure from the north against the open flank of the Regiment became stronger and stronger. Enemy troops attacked with twelve heavy tanks and infantry. SS-Sturmbannführer Weidinger immediately came to the daring decision to attack with all available forces to the north in order to make possible the disengagement of our own troops from the pocket. Leading in the foremost line, SS-Sturmbannführer Weidinger took the hill St. Leger with his brave Regiment. Again and again his untiring dash and example with his leadership excited the men to the highest actions of bravery. In a bitter battle the hill was conquered, seven tanks were destroyed, and the following enemy attack was unmercifully beaten. The Regimental Commander made the decision to hold the attained positions with all available means in order to prevent a new closing of the pocket. All continuous enemy attacks fought with superior forces are being destroyed in a stubborn struggle. Four Sherman tanks were demolished.

SS-Sturmbannführer Weidinger personally lead the counterattack and his command inflicted heavy and bloody losses on the enemy. At 6:15 pm the Regiment announced to the Division that the road is being held open and that our own forces are pouring out of the pocket. More than 4,000 soldiers, including 300 officers and three Generals from all services, as well as more than 800 vehicles of all types, marched on the attack road of the Regiment during the night. This superior-level accomplishment of the remnants of SS-Regiment 'Der Führer' can be traced back most of all to the outstanding bravery and power of determination of the Regimental Commander. With constant severity against himself, he swept his men along to the highest accomplishment, performance of duty, and enthusiasm."[42]

Following the withdrawal to Germany, temporary Divisional Commander and Swords holder SS-Oberführer Otto Baum submitted an application on September 5, 1944, for Weidinger to be promoted to SS-Obersturmbannführer. This, his last official promotion, was approved and became effective November 9, 1944. Baum's recommendation included the comment:

"Clean and clear character with an open and honest personality. Mentally gifted above average. Marked soldierly appearance with pleasant manners. Decorated with the Knight's Cross with Oakleaves for highest achievements in the field. Weidinger fills his position as Regimental Commander with great success despite the short time he has held the post."[43]

On September 27, 1944, Weidinger was wounded for the fourth time when an anti-vehicle mine detonated, injuring his face and head as well as damaging an ear drum. Following a short respite and refit from the summer 1944 combats in France, "Das Reich" was readied as a component of the final offensive in the west, the Ardennes Offensive or Battle of the Bulge. "Das Reich," including Weidinger's troops, was assigned to II.SS-Panzer-Korps for the December, 1944, start of the battle. At this time Weidinger's Regiment was composed as follows:

[42] "Vorschlag Nr. 4 für die Verleihung des Eichenlaubes zum Ritterkreuz des Eisernen Kreuzes" dated November 30, 1944, and signed by Heinz Lammerding.

[43] 2.SS-Pz. Div "Das Reich," "Personal-Antrag," dated September 5, 1944, and signed by Otto Baum.

SS-Panzer-Grenadier-Regiment 4 "Der Führer"
commander: SS-Obersturmbannführer Otto Weidinger
adjutant: SS-Hauptsturmführer Georg Seegerer[44]

Regimentsstab (regimental staff)
Stabskompanie (Staff Company, numbered the 17th)
Nachrichtenzug (signals platoon)
Kraderkundungszug (motorcycle dispatch platoon)

I.Bataillon (battalion)
battalion commander: SS-Sturmbannführer Karl Götsche[45]
Stab (staff)
Nachrichtenzug (signals platoon)
1.Panzergrenadier Kompanie (armoured infantry company)
2.Panzergrenadier Kompanie
3.Panzergrenadier Kompanie
4.(schwere) Kompanie (heavy company)
Versorgungskompanie (support and supply company)

II.Bataillon
battalion commander: SS-Hauptsturmführer Hans Schulzer[46]
Stab
Nachrichtenzug
5.Panzergrenadier Kompanie
6.Panzergrenadier Kompanie
7.Panzergrenadier Kompanie
8.(schwere) Kompanie
Versorgungskompanie

III.Bataillon (armoured battalion with half-tracked vehicles)
battalion commander: SS-Sturmbannführer Heinz Werner[47]
Stab
Nachrichtenzug
9.Schützenpanzerwagen Kompanie (armoured personnel carrier company)
10.Schützenpanzerwagen Kompanie
11.Schützenpanzerwagen Kompanie
12.(schwere) Kompanie
Versorgungskompanie

13.Kompanie (sIG-Kompanie) (supporting infantry gun company)
14.Kompanie (Flak-Kompanie) (supporting anti-aircraft company)
16.Kompanie (Pionier-Kompanie) (supporting engineer company)

Weidinger was awarded the Oakleaves to the Knight's Cross one day after it had been formally approved on December 27th. According to II.SS-Panzer-Korps commander and Swords to the Knight's Cross bearer Wilhelm Bittrich, the award took place as follows:

> *"During the Ardennes Offensive, after heavy fighting in the early morning hours of December 28, 1944, the two Regimental commanders, SS-Obersturmbannführer Günther Wisliceny of SS-Regiment 'Deutschland' and SS-Obersturmbannführer Otto Weidinger of SS-Regiment 'Der Führer,' were ordered to the Divisional of Headquarters of 'Das Reich' in the chateau St. Jean, where the commander of the 6.SS-Panzer-Armee, Sepp Dietrich, had already arrived. He awarded SS-Obersturmbannführer Günther Wisliceny as the 687th, and SS-Obersturmbannführer Otto Weidinger as the 688th soldiers of the German Armed Forces, the Oakleaves of the Knight's Cross of the Iron Cross for their leadership on the invasion front. SS-Obersturmbannführer Weidinger received this high decoration for the vital counterattack to open and keep open the Falaise pocket, in which the 7th Army under SS-Oberst-Gruppenführer Paul Hausser was encircled."*[48]

Following the losses incurred during the Ardennes offensive, "Das Reich" was reinforced with whatever replacements were available. Although the Western front was in a situation of near-collapse, in January, 1945, Hitler ordered Sepp Dietrich's 6.SS-Panzer-Armee to organize an offensive to help relieve the units which were trapped in Hungary, especially the SS Cavalry Divisions trapped in Budapest. Delays in relo-

[44] Seegerer succeeded Heinz Werner as adjutant on June 9, 1944, when the latter assumed his battalion command. He held the adjutant post until the end of the war and, in May 1945, was awarded the German Cross in Gold.
[45] Götsche led the II./Der Führer from the end of October 1944 until mid-March 1945.
[46] Won the German Cross in Gold on September 26, 1944, for leadership of the 5./Der Führer as an SS-Obersturmführer.
[47] Wounded on December 24, 1944, he returned to his command and led the III./Der Führer until the end of the war. Werner died on August 9, 1978.

[48] Letter from Wilhelm Bittrich to Otto Weidinger dated June 17, 1966.

cation and insufficient numbers found the attack to free the encircled troops doomed from the beginning. Weidinger's 3rd Battalion under the command of SS-Sturmbannführer Heinz Werner engaged in especially severe combat in and around Heinrich major. Werner, as commander of the armored III./Der Führer, won the Oakleaves to the Knight's Cross. Though difficult to restrict a selection to one officer, Herr Weidinger felt that Heinz Werner was among the finest commanders who served under him during the war.

Weidinger's unit retreated across the Austrian border and attempted to defend Vienna. Against overwhelming odds the combat for the canal area was as much for survival as tactical gain. The last bridge to defend was the Floridsdorfer and the battles to hold it were the most severe of the final months of the war. Though Weidinger realized the war was lost, he continued to follow orders and fight, exactly as any soldier in any country would. Under the commander of the troops in Vienna, General der Infanterie Rudolf von Bünau, the area was held for several days despite overwhelming odds. But by April 13, 1945, Weidinger's command and the other German forces had pulled out of the Austrian capital.

In 1945, "Das Reich" had several different commanders. One of these, probably SS-Standartenführer Rudolf Lehmann, submitted an application for Weidinger to be awarded the Swords to the Knight's Cross. The telex didn't survive the war for study, but it is probable that Weidinger's defense of Vienna was at least partly responsible for his being nominated for the award. The recommendation was approved on May 6, 1945, as the 150th Swords to be given out among all the services. At this late date communications were near impossible. Many later awards, among them Weidinger's Swords, were unknown to the recipients themselves.

During the final months, many promotions were submitted and many were actually approved. However, only those who had their notification prior to the surrender were actually able to attain the new rank. Most of these were unknown to the officers themselves and such was the case with the promotion to SS-Standartenführer which was recommended for Weidinger. In the author's opinion, confirmed by numerous veteran and historian correspondences, there is little doubt that Weidinger would have obtained a higher level command had the war progressed.

With the end of the war in sight, the various units of "Das Reich" pulled back from the Russian forces in an attempt to escape the inevitable fate of Soviet captivity. In the confusion of late April 1945, the various units of "Das Reich" were dispersed. Weidinger's unit was in the Budweis area and on May 1, 1945, Weidinger was ordered to report to the German commander of Prague. There he met Princess Stephan zu Schaumburg-Lippe who had the task of organizing the evacuation of wounded and German civilians from the capital. Unlike many units, Weidinger's SS-Regiment "Der Führer" was fully armed and capable of offensive or defensive action. On May 5th "Der Führer" was placed with those units under the command of Feldmarschall Ferdinand Schörner as it was impossible for the regiment to rejoin the main body of "Das Reich."[49] The unit was ordered directly to Prague where, on May 8, 1945, Weidinger's men stormed the Troya bridge. On this date, the surrender was announced and, taking all wounded and civilians with them, "Der Führer" left the Czech capital and moved towards Pilsen. On May 9, 1945, Weidinger made contact with the U.S. 2nd Infantry Division near Rokiczany. After ordering his unit to destroy its major weapons, he entered captivity with the men of his regiment.

Imprisoned longer than normal for an officer innocent of any war crimes, Weidinger was held in numerous military and civilian camps starting with the police barracks in Klattau. He was then moved for periods as a Prisoner-of-War to Camp 22 in Regensburg until mid-November, 1945, then Camp 430 in Landshut until the end of June, 1946. Weidinger was next held in civil prison, still awaiting a fair trial, in Regensburg, Kornwestheim, Asperg, Ludwigsburg, Reutlingen, Hohenasperg and Dachau until August 1947 when he was handed over to French authorities in Bordeaux. He was held by the French, along with other members of "Das Reich," into 1951. This lengthy incarceration was due to the events involving the Division on the way to Normandy near the village of Tulle and Oradour-sur-Glane. His wife, Anneliese, traveled by train in post-war ravaged Germany to visit her husband whenever possible while he was incarcerated. Finally tried by the French in the summer of 1951, Weidinger was found innocent of all charges and released in June, 1951.

---

[49] Schörner became a Feldmarschall in April 1945. He won the Knight's Cross on April 20, 1941, as a Generalmajor commanding the 6.Gebirgs-Division. On February 17, 1944, as a General der Gebirgstruppen, he was awarded the Oakleaves as commander of the XXXX.Panzer-Korps. Leading Heeresgruppe "Nord" (Army Group "North") as a Generaloberst, he won the Swords on August 28, 1944. At that same rank and command, he became the 23rd soldier awarded the Diamonds on January 1, 1945. Captured in 1945, he did not return from Russian captivity until 1955.

I asked Herr Weidinger when he first heard of his Swords decoration, as notice was not received in the chaos of May 1945:

> *"When I returned home on June 24, 1951, after six-and-a-half years of captivity and acquittal by the Higher Military Court in Bordeaux France, my last commander, SS-Standartenführer Rudolf Lehmann, wrote me a letter on September 1, 1951. In this he said, 'By the way, do you know yet that you were awarded the Swords ? For this, in spite of everything, my heartiest congratulations. I learned about it from Hermann Buch, who in turn found out from Wilhelm Kment, as our representative on the OKH PA 3.'"*[50]

At the start of October, 1951, Weidinger began a new education to become a pharmacist, passing his license examination two years later. He assumed operations of his father-in-law's business in Aalen in June, 1953. Established in 1928, the family business later expanded to several stores in the Aalen area. Weidinger worked continuously and did not retire until the age of 72. He wrote numerous articles regarding his units and was among the earliest and most active leaders of the "Der Führer" and "Das Reich" veterans associations. With much hard work his career prospered and the joys of family life came after many difficult years of waiting. A son, Wolfgang, was born on June 18, 1954.

In 1962, Otto Weidinger finished compiling the history of SS-Regiment "Der Führer" titled "Kameraden bis zum Ende" (*Comrades to the End*). Following this, at the request of Paul Hausser, came nearly two decades of research needed to complete the six volume official history of "Das Reich" which was released between 1967 and 1982. Both these standard works are highly recommended for all military historians In 1986, he wrote a study of the events in France that had resulted in his post-war internment, "Tulle and Oradour, a Franco-German Tragedy." As an honored member of the Association of Knight's Cross Bearers, Weidinger continued to aid historians of his former units as well pursuing his own studies on the same topic. On April 23, 1983, he became honorary head of the "Das Reich" veterans group, having led the regimental veteran association for Regiment "Der Führer" since its establishment.

Nature walks and preserving flowers allowed him relaxation while his interest in history continued. Aiding authors and researchers from many countries, he also enjoyed reading ancient to modern history, as well as being well-versed in the complete history of Aalen where he lived.

With great joy, he lived long enough to see the reunification of Germany following the fall of the Berlin Wall in November 1989. Herr Weidinger was responsible for this author having the privilege to meet many veteran commanders and high award winners from "Das Reich" and other Waffen-SS units. Most importantly, he helped acquire support for my continued research of his former units until his death after a brief illness on January 10, 1990, a few months before his 50th wedding anniversary. At the following meeting of veterans of Regiment "Der Führer," in October, 1990, the association took his name as its honor title.

The personal character and contributions of a man can be fully judged after his death. As a soldier who fought for his country with distinction, Otto Weidinger followed that most intense period of life with a successful civilian career and a treasured family life. His historical contributions, as a writer/historian as well as assisting colleagues and researchers alike, are possibly the most important legacies he left to those interested in the Second World War. To this author, Otto Weidinger was a much admired and trusted friend, possessing the most honorable character of anyone I've known. He will always be fondly remembered and admired by those who knew him personally or professionally.

[50] Letter to the author from Herr Weidinger dated January 2, 1987. Hermann Buch was the last divisional adjutant (IIa) of "Das Reich."

In his first photo in uniform, Otto Weidinger displays the collar insignia designating the 56.SS-Standarte. His visor hat shows early style insignia and, though not shown, the uniform included a sleeve title with the number designation of the Standarte as well.

Wearing the rank of SS-Standartenjunker, Weidinger is shown with "B" collar insignia in this formal portrait taken while attending SS-Führerschule Braunschweig during late 1935.

Two views of the Braunschweig facility. In the upper photo, the first class of SS cadets are lined to hear visiting senior officers on June 30, 1935.

(Above) Himmler, Friedrich Jeckeln, Karl Wolff and Walter Schmitt are among the SS General rank officers attending the graduation of the first cadet class from Braunschweig. Note other guests from various branches of the military are at left. Below, the same General rank officers salute at the end of ceremonies.

The swimming hall at Braunschweig is seen above. Below, Weidinger is shown in the observation area of the statue atop the main building during a wartime visit.

Paul Hausser (with helmet), Himmler and Wolff inspect the graduates. On the left: a stairwell inside the school during August 1935, previously an Army cadet facility with a lengthy history. The building itself was destroyed in a 1944 air attack.

The mess hall at Ellwangen is shown above and, left, the pre-war barracks of SS-Regiment "Deutschland."

During engineer training (above), Weidinger is 2nd from left at Sennelager during October 1935. All training is done with ties and in full service uniform. Note the SS/VT overseas caps. Below are Hans Weiss (2nd from left), Karl Heuer (3rd from left, later a Sturmbannführer in the Hauptamt Ordnungspolizei), Otto Weidinger (4th from left) and Friedrich Hengstmann (killed in April 1945 as an SS-Sturmbannführer on the staff of the XI.SS-Panzer-Korps). A variety of uniforms are being worn, all showing the "Deutschland" honor title on the left sleeve.

Otto Weidinger in black dress uniform wearing his SS sword as an SS-Untersturmführer and in a gray service uniform, both just after being commissioned. In the photo at left, Weidinger (front left) leads a parade formation with dress sword presented.

A formal portrait of Weidinger in dress black uniform with "SS 1" collar tab as an SS-Untersturmführer.

Two views of SS-Untersturmführer Weidinger (above) show him with "SS 1" collar tab on his coat and a signed photo in black uniform. Below left, Weidinger (left with field cap) and men of the reconnaissance unit enjoy candy from home during the 1940 French campaign. Note the black uniform with Panzer beret. Georg Seegerer, Weidinger's adjutant with SS-Regiment "Der Führer," is at lower right.

The author's favorite pre-war portrait. Otto Weidinger's greatcoat does not show the "1" collar designation but does display the "Deutschland" cufftitle. He wears an Army pattern sword and officer's visor cap.

Walter Krüger leads a battalion colors formation of IV./Deutschland in the upper photo. Weidinger is nearest the camera (left) beside Krüger and wears the stylized "D" regimental cipher on his shoulder board.

Krüger (right, with Otto Weidinger when both served in "Deutschland." Below, Krüger is in front of the Ellwangen battalion color guard. Walter Krüger was among the best Waffen-SS senior commanders, commanding "Das Reich" during 1943 before winning the Knight's Cross with Oakleaves and Swords in 1945 as an SS-Obergruppenführer commanding a corps.

Weidinger's full length portrait for his eventual marriage application. In the February 1937 group photo in Ellwangen are, from left, Karl Gesele (Knight's Cross as an SS-Obersturmbannführer in command of the SS-Sturmbrigade "Reichsführer-SS" on July 4, 1944), Fritz Schott (signals officer for III./Deutschland and later an SS-Sturmbannführer), Walter Plöw (German Cross in Gold on January 13, 1945, as an SS-Obersturmbannführer commanding SS-Flak Abteilung 11), Weidinger, unknown, Hans Bollert (later a company commander in "Der Führer" and in 1944 as an SS-Sturmbannführer commanded I./Panzer Regiment 9).

Weidinger (above and below right) training with his cross-country pack team. Below left is Hans Weiss, later winner of the Knight's Cross on April 6, 1943, for leadership of the reconnaissance detachment of "Das Reich." He was also awarded the German Cross in Gold on April 23, 1944, for service with the "Das Reich" motorcycle battalion during 1941-1943 and then led a Tiger tank detachment.

Weidinger's pack marching team with "Deutschland" competed often in the pre-war years. In Dresden during 1937, Weidinger and Weiss lead the formation at left and a photographer runs along side. Below, Weidinger marching beside the formation. With full pack, they marched 25 kilometers in three hours, 35 minutes and 55 seconds. Though somewhat smaller in stature, Weidinger set the march pace for the team.

Weidinger (above with visor cap) with some of his subordinates at the Hamburg zoo. At left, during a 1937 leave in Ellwangen are (from left) Walter Plöw, Paul Massell (later an SS-Obersturmbannführer and regimental commander), Hans Bissinger (German Cross in Gold on April 24, 1943, with "Deutschland") and Weidinger. Plöw wears an SS sword while Weidinger wears an Army pattern saber.

Otto Weidinger at the 1936 Nuremberg Rally. He is in black dress uniform on the right speaking with his brother, Hans Weidinger (center) who then served with a Totenkopf unit.

A color guard (above) shows, from right, Weidinger, Fritz Sabel and Hans Weiss. Mounted on the horse is later "Leibstandarte" 1a, Erich Grensing. With Weidinger in the center, front row (below) is his marching team at the 1937 Party Day Rally in Nuremberg.

The cross-country pack team of IV./Deutschland with Weidinger (front row, center) prior to the 1938 Hamburg competition wearing full packs with rifles. Below (from left) during mid-1941 are Weidinger, Ferdinand Tietz (commander of the "Reich" engineer battalion), Friedrich-Karl Dermietzel (divisional surgeon, awarded the German Cross in Silver on June 2, 1944, and ended the war as senior medical officer of the 6.SS-Panzer-Armee).

Weidinger in a portrait wearing Army uniform during the late autumn of 1938. His tunic and cap are piped in white for infantry.

Two views of the pre-war honor guard of the Aufklärungsabteilung SS/VT. The rarely seen unit patch of the reconnaissance colors, SS AA, can be seen. Otto Weidinger is nearest the camera above and commander Dr. Wilhelm Brandt is on the far left in the lower photo next to Weidinger.

Weidinger (wearing white gloves) commands the honor guard during a visit by Hitler.

SS-Obersturmführer Otto Weidinger after his November 1939 award of the Iron Cross 2nd class following the Polish campaign.

Men of the Reconnaissance Detachment celebrating after awards of the Iron Cross 2nd class in 1939. Back row from left are Dr. Hans Siebrecht (detachment doctor, later divisional doctor of the 18.SS-Freiwilligen-Panzer-Grenadier-Division "Horst Wessel"), Kurt Pachur (2.Kompanie Chef), Hans Weiss, Otto Weidinger (adjutant), Herbert Oeck (platoon leader, later commander of SS-Panzer-Grenadier-Regiment 9), Heinrich Wulf (in 1944 reconnaissance commander for "Das Reich"), Theodor Schnabel, Karl-Otto Schlei, Karl Heuer (administrative officer), Fritz Vogt (first Knight's Cross holder of the unit, awarded the Oakleaves with the 17.SS-Panzer-Grenadier-Division "Götz von Berlichingen" in 1945). Front row from left are Dr. Wilhelm Brandt (commander), Herbert Kuhlmann (Knight's Cross on February 13, 1944, while with the Panzer Regiment of "Hitlerjugend"), Dr. Peter Liebrich (later "Leibstandarte" divisional surgeon), Werner Poetschke (Knight's Cross with Oakleaves with the "Leibstandarte" Panzer Regiment) and Kurt Preusser (signals officer).

Shown above are recruits for the armored car component of the reconnaissance unit in Holland during 1940. Weidinger is seated in gray uniform. In the lower photo, Weidinger (right) eats with Werner Poetschke in 1940.

Above, from right, are reconnaissance men Kurt Preusser, Karl-Otto Schlei, Otto Weidinger, Dr. Wilhelm Brandt, Hans Weiss and Dr. Hans Siebricht. Weidinger stands in the center of the lower photo with armored car personnel. 2nd from the left is later Panzer Regiment "Das Reich" 5th Company commander and German Cross in Gold holder Karl-Heinz Himme.

Weidinger (above right) and Dr. Wilhelm Brandt award 2nd class Iron Crosses in Leerdamm, Holland to the 1st Company in August 1940 after the Western campaign. Below, Weidinger stands at left with his men after the ceremony.

The same ceremony period as previously shown sees (above, from left) Weidinger, Hans-Henning Heuer (medical officer of the 1st Company) and Christian Tychsen (3rd Company commander, later Knight's Cross with Oakleaves as "Das Reich" Panzer Regiment commander). On the left, a signed photo shows commander Brandt awarding Weidinger the Iron Cross 1st class.

Otto Weidinger is seen above right with Karl Heuer, the administrative officer of the divisional reconnaissance component. At left, Weidinger is seen standing left on top of his company commander's eight-wheeled armored car.

SS-Hauptsturmführer Otto Weidinger after his award of the Iron Cross 1st class while assigned to the divisional staff as intelligence officer.

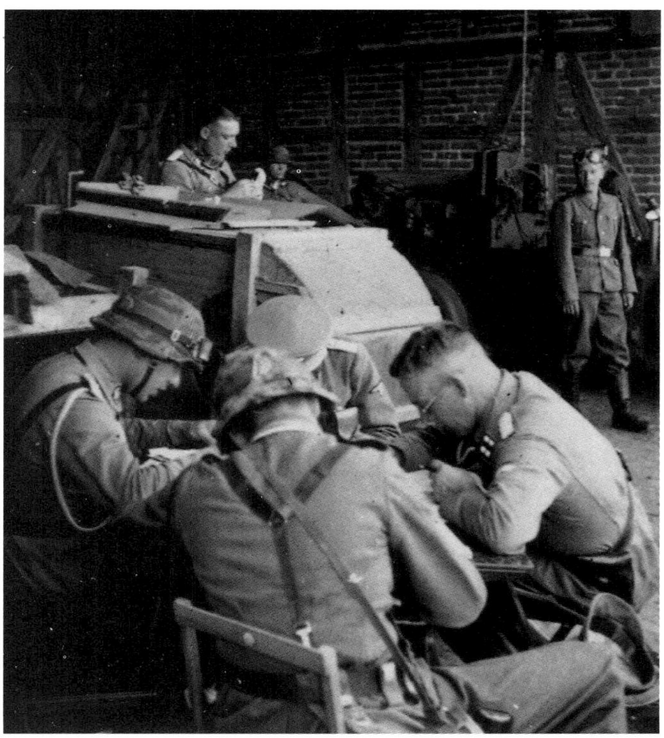

In East Prussia during training in the summer of 1939, above, from left are Dr. Wilhelm Brandt, Hans Weiss and Weidinger. On the left: seated at left is Weidinger and on the right is reconnaissance commander Brandt.

Above on the far right is Otto Kröger and beside him is Otto Weidinger while both served with the staff on April 20, 1941. At left, Weidinger recovers from his summer 1941 wound while divisional adjutant.

Two views of Weidinger during mid-April 1941 in Yugoslavia. "Reich" captured Belgrade and brought a quick end to the campaign.

"Reich" divisional staff officers in Yugoslavia during 1941 are, above from left, Dr. Ernst Schäfer, Otto Weidinger, Erwin Mix (then an ordnance officer, later II.SS-Panzer-Korps intelligence officer), Otto Kröger and Aurel Kowatsch (killed in 1945 as "Das Reich" intelligence officer). Below, Weidinger is in the center. On the far right is Otto Kröger who was killed on November 29, 1941, while commanding III./Deutschland.

Clockwise from above left are a 1941 image of Weidinger while sightseeing, a signed photo as an SS-Obersturmführer and while in Vesoul during 1941 serving as divisional adjutant.

Pages 57-58: Four consecutive photos show Weidinger while instructing cadets in tactics and leading a march at SS-Junkerschule Braunschweig in 1942. In this war-time period the cadets do not show the pre-war "B" collar insignia being worn.

Upon his return in early 1943 to "Das Reich," Weidinger (left) speaks with SS-Generalkommando leader Paul Hausser (right) during lunch. The Sturmbannführer facing the camera is Otto Hansmann (formerly commander of III./Deutschland and then assigned to the corps staff) and with back to camera is Hauptmann Raecke (field police commander of "Das Reich"). Weidinger is also seen at left during the autumn of 1943 in Russia.

Heinrich Himmler congratulates members of the division his spring visit of 1943 after Kharkov. Himmler is shaking hands with eventual 16./Deutschland Knight's Cross holder Alois Weber while war reporters record the event. Weidinger is 3rd from left. At left, Weidinger (right) is shown with Walter Drexler (hands folded, commander of the 4th Company) after the heavy tank battle at Kolomak on September 12, 1943. Drexler won the Knight's Cross as reconnaissance commander of the 8.SS-Kavallerie-Division "Florian Geyer" on December 11, 1944.

Otto Weidinger (right) and Walter Drexler after the fierce Kolomak battles in September 1943. Drexler served with the reconnaissance unit from early 1941 to mid-1944. He held the rank of SS-Obersturmbannführer when killed in February 1945, with "Florian Geyer."

Weidinger (in passenger seat) discusses an autumn 1943 reconnaissance mission with his adjutant, Hans Prix (standing left). Prix was killed the last day of 1943. At left, Weidinger points during a visit with heavy reconnaissance company commander Walter Drexler in September 1943.

Wearing his German Cross in Gold, Weidinger poses with officers of the Battle Group in 1944. Far left is Hans-Joachim Fuchs (battalion medical officer) then Hans Hentschel (signals officer). The wounded man is ordnance officer Karl-Heinz Buchwald. Below, Weidinger (7th from left) with Battle Group officers just prior to leaving Russia. 4th from left is Walter Ludwig (company officer), 6th from left Dr. Ernst Müller (Battle Group medical officer), 5th from right with German Cross is Hans Eckert (battalion commander and later "Deutschland" Knight's Cross holder) and 3rd from right is Ernst Gerwig (adjutant).

"Das Reich" commander Heinz Lammerding (right in both photos) welcomes Weidinger and the Battle Group upon their return from the Russian front.

Lammerding (upper photo, standing right) talks with Weidinger after awarding him the Knight's Cross. Lammerding, previously commander of the Battle Group, won his Knight's Cross for that command. Weidinger's award came from combats while leading the reconnaissance detachment in 1943. Below, two casual photos taken by his men after the award.

Clockwise from top left: Weidinger (right) with Heinz Lammerding and SS-Regiment "Der Führer" commander Sylvester Stadler after the ceremony. Weidinger, wearing his new Knight's Cross, relaxes with Dr. Gerhard Rueff. Rueff served as senior doctor of several units including the motorcycle battalion, reconnaissance detachment and assault gun components of "Das Reich." A casual pose wearing a field cap shows that Weidinger did not always wear his German Cross though the tunic shown as no loops for the badge.

A new holder of the Knight's Cross was honored often when they returned from the front. A spring 1944 celebration presents Weidinger in Niedermarzbürg. Honor guards display colors and members of several organizations can be seen, including the Hitler Youth. Below, Weidinger salutes a memorial to veterans killed in World War I.

A formal portrait of Weidinger wearing an officer's visor hat displays his decorations. Included are the Close Combat Clasp, ribbon bar, Iron Cross 1st class, Wound Badge in Silver, Infantry Assault Badge, German Cross in Gold and Knight's Cross. His new tunic does not yet have a "Das Reich" sleeve title.

Weidinger is reunited with his wife, Anneliese, in Aalen when allowed a leave after the award of the Knight's Cross. In the top photo, from left, are the mayor of Aalen, Frau Weidinger, Otto Weidinger and the NSDAP district leader, Kreisleiter Kölle. Weidinger is then being congratulated by members of the civil community.

Weidinger presents medals to men of the Battle Group after his award of the Knight's Cross. Below, the first posed photo of him wearing his new decoration.

Taken in Aalen, a portrait shows Otto Weidinger just prior to returning to "Das Reich."

The Knight's Cross is formally awarded to Heinz Werner (5th from left) on September 2, 1944. To the left of Werner is "Das Reich" commander and later Swords holder Otto Baum while Otto Weidinger is to the right. A portrait of Werner, awarded the Oakleaves and the Close Combat Clasp in Gold. He was Weidinger's favorite subordinate commander in SS-Regiment "Der Führer."

The above autumn 1944 photos show Weidinger in camouflage jacket. He wears only his Knight's Cross and Iron Cross with just shoulder boards to designate his rank. No sleeve title for SS-Regiment "Der Führer" is worn with this style uniform. As often seen, he does not wear his German Cross as it attracted attention in the field. The award document for that decoration was lost when Weidinger's command vehicle was destroyed in Russia. It was one of the few decorations he managed to keep after the war. Damaged during the war, the award was restored and given to him on his 75th birthday by his wife and children.

Otto Weidinger and his adjutant, Georg Seegerer, decorate men of SS-Panzer-Grenadier-Regiment 4 "Der Führer" after the Normandy battles.

Otto Weidinger in an informal pose, away from the front, with all his awards. He wears his officer's hat with chin cord but, as seen in combat area photos, preferred other styles of headgear in the field.

(Above) Weidinger (in helmet) with III./Der Führer commander Heinz Werner in Austria during 1945. At left, during the same period, Weidinger wears his final rank of SS-Obersturmbannführer and the Oakleaves to the Knight's Cross.

Shown above left is this author's favorite wartime portrait. Weidinger is next in the center with Heinz Werner (left) and Georg Seegerer. At left, he is in the "Der Führer" headquarters during 1945.

Weidinger (above left) with Georg Seegerer and below the pair again discuss a rare light moment during the heavy fighting in Austria in 1945.

Georg Seegerer and Weidinger stand to the right of a regimental headquarters vehicle (note tactical symbol). At left are Weidinger (with helmet) and General der Infanterie Rudolf von Bünau (Knight's Cross). Both photos taken during the final phase of the war in Vienna, Austria.

After the war Otto Weidinger was an honored member of the Organization of Knight's Cross holders. Above left, he attends their meeting in 1986 and is on vacation the same year at right. At left, Weidinger sits at right with Hans Hauser (Knight's Cross in 1945 with SS-Regiment "Der Führer").

Otto Weidinger at a meeting of Knight's Cross holders in 1984. Of the 17 men awarded the Knight's Cross while with SS-Regiment "Der Führer," only Weidinger received the Swords while assigned to that unit. Sylvester Stadler, Otto Kumm and Heinz Werner also received the Oakleaves during service with "Der Führer." Stadler and Kumm won their Swords during later assignments.

Der Reichsführer-SS

Berlin, den 5. Mai 1936.

SS-Standartenoberjunker

W e i d i n g e r , Otto

(SS-Nr. 114 921 - III/SS Deutschland)
der SS-Verfügungstruppe.

Ich befördere Sie zum: SS-Untersturmführer

Tag der Beförderung ist der: 20. April 1936.

Der Reichsführer-SS

i. A.

Heissmeyer

Nationalsoz. Deutsche Arbeiterpartei * Der Reichsführer SS *

Formal promotion document given to Otto Weidinger when commissioned as an SS-Untersturmführer. Showing his initial posting, the signature is that of August Heissmeyer.

Der Führer und Reichskanzler

hat aus Anlaß der Wiedervereinigung
Österreichs mit dem Deutschen Reich

dem

SS-Untersturmführer

Otto Weidinger

die

Medaille zur Erinnerung
an den 13. März 1938

verliehen.

Berlin, den 2. März 1939

Der Staatsminister
und Chef der Präsidialkanzlei
des Führers und Reichskanzlers

Meissner

Award document for the March 13, 1938, medal given for the annexation of Austria. The signature is State Secretary and Minister of the Presidential Chancellery, Dr. Otto Meissner.

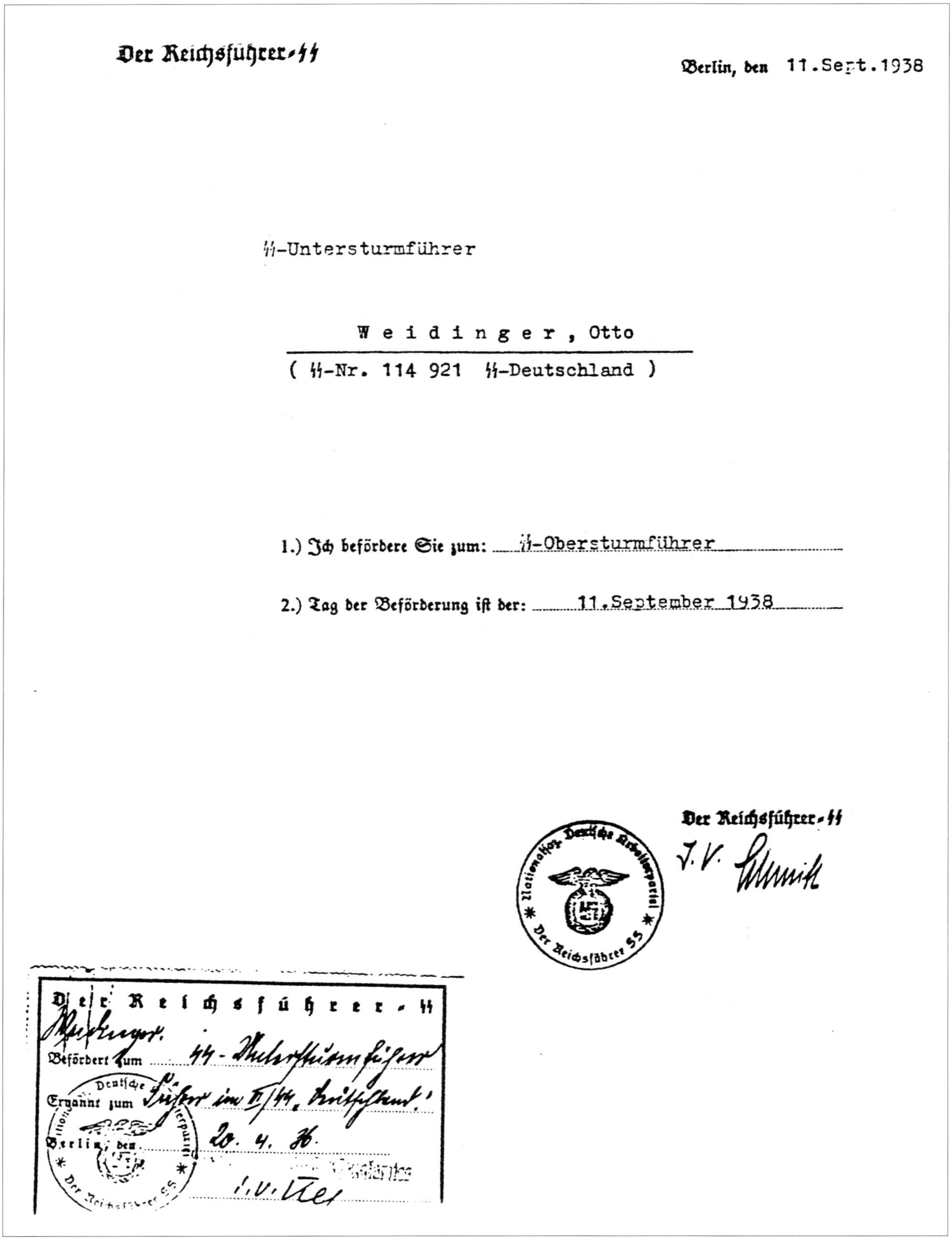

Der Reichsführer-SS

Berlin, den 11.Sept.1938

SS-Untersturmführer

W e i d i n g e r , Otto

(SS-Nr. 114 921 SS-Deutschland)

1.) Ich befördere Sie zum: SS-Obersturmführer

2.) Tag der Beförderung ist der: 11.September 1938

Der Reichsführer-SS

I.V. Schmitt

Nationalsoz. Deutsche Arbeiterpartei * Der Reichsführer SS *

Der Reichsführer-SS

Weidinger

Befördert zum SS-Untersturmführer

Ernannt zum

Berlin, den 20. 4. 36.

Promotion document for Otto Weidinger advancing him in rank to SS-Obersturmführer, signed by Walter Schmitt.

Im Namen des Führers
und Oberſten Befehlshabers
der Wehrmacht

verleihe ich

dem

SS-Obersturmführer

Otto Weidinger

das

Eiſerne Kreuz 2. Klaſſe.

............Pilsen....., den.....15.11........1939

(Dienſtſiegel)

(Dienſtgrad und Dienſtſtellung)

SS-Gruppenführer u.

Div. Kdr.

Otto Weidinger's Iron Cross 2nd class document signed by Paul Hausser.

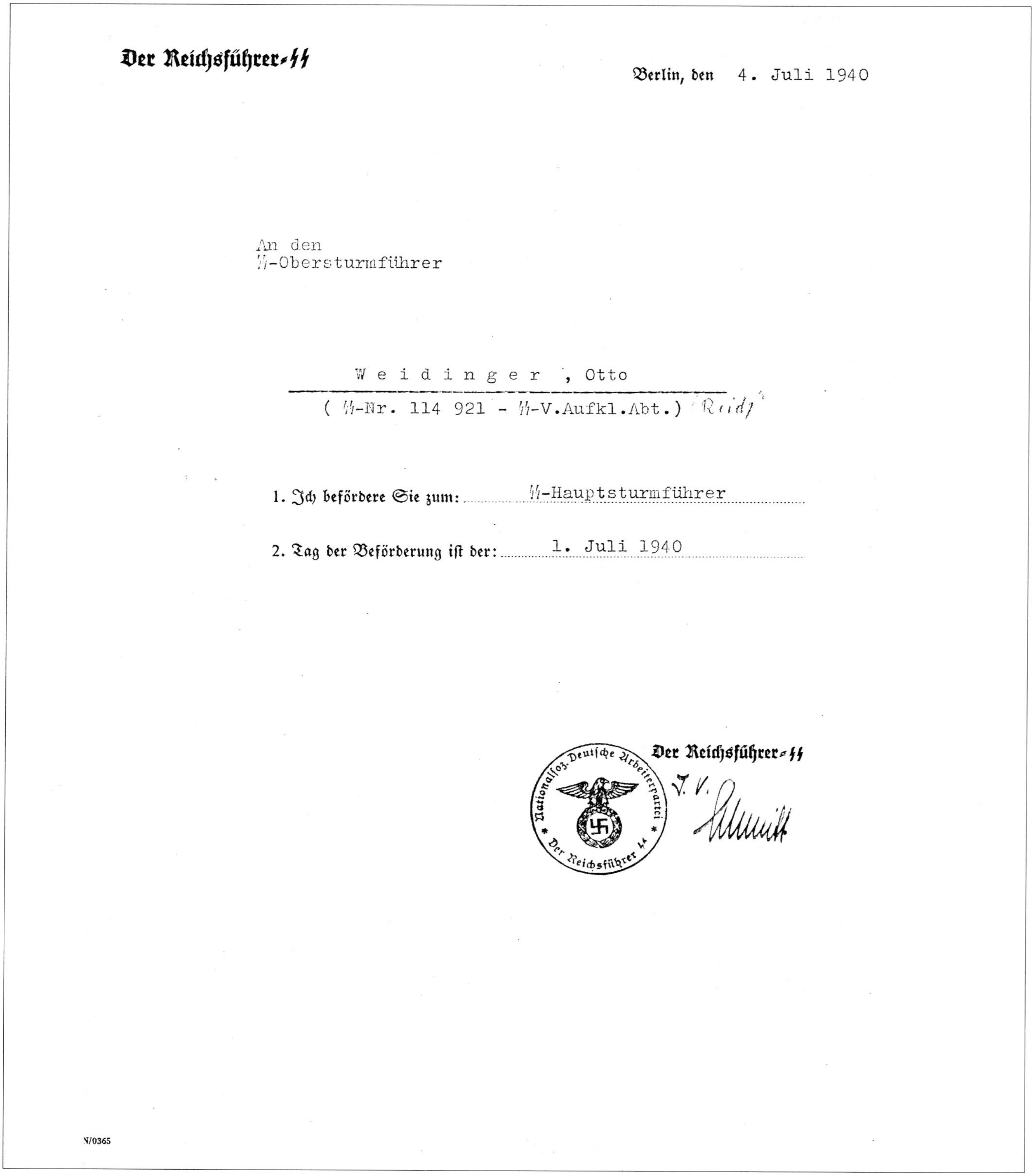

Der Reichsführer-SS

Berlin, den 4. Juli 1940

An den
SS-Obersturmführer

Weidinger, Otto
(SS-Nr. 114 921 - SS-V.Aufkl.Abt.)

1. Ich befördere Sie zum: SS-Hauptsturmführer

2. Tag der Beförderung ist der: 1. Juli 1940

Der Reichsführer-SS
I.V. Schmitt

V/0365

Formal promotion document to SS-Hauptsturmführer while assigned to the reconnaissance Detachment, again signed by Walter Schmitt.

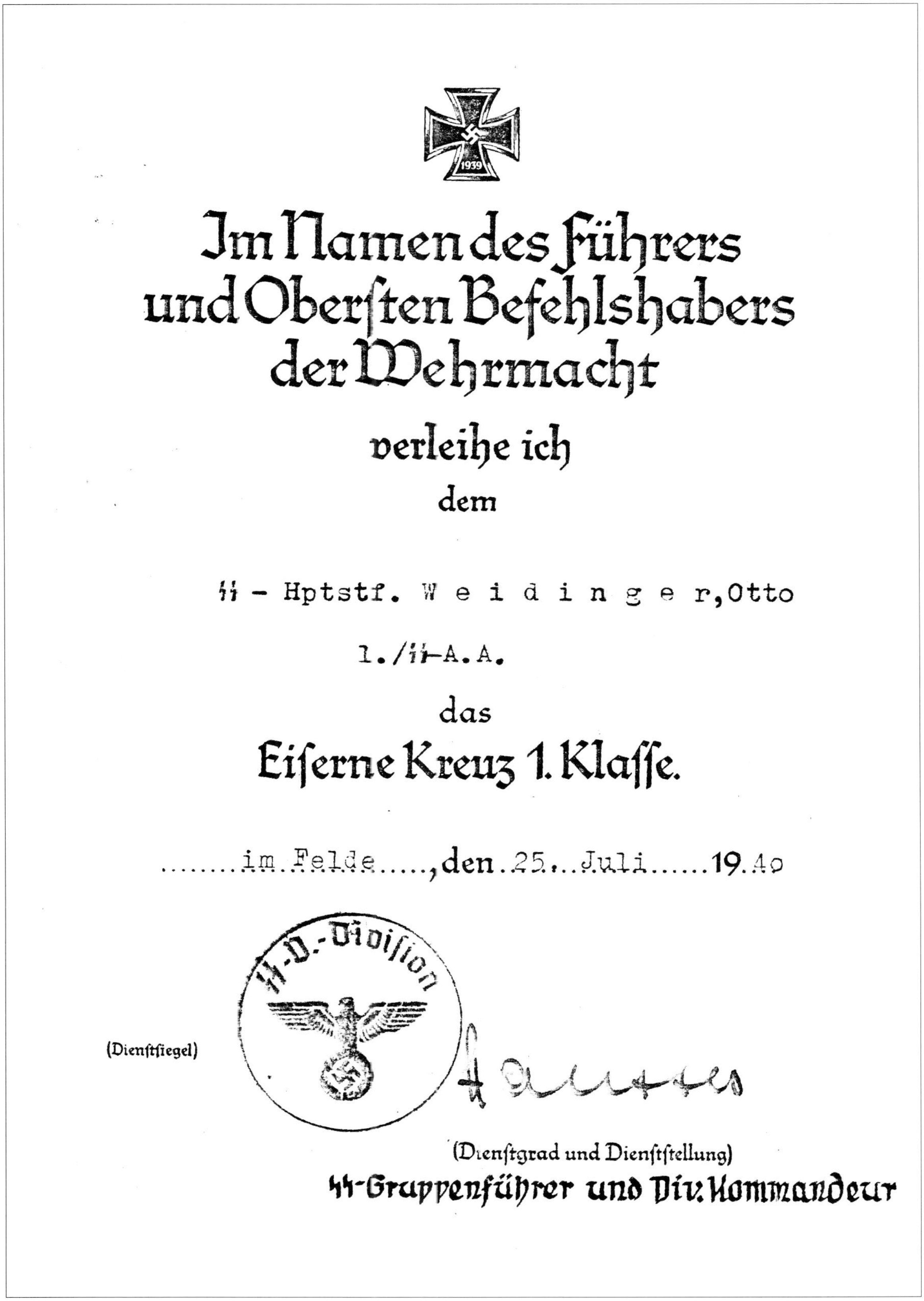

1939

Im Namen des Führers und Obersten Befehlshabers der Wehrmacht

verleihe ich

dem

SS - Hptstf. W e i d i n g e r, Otto

1./SS-A.A.

das

Eiserne Kreuz 1. Klasse.

........im Felde.....,den..25...Juli......19.40

SS-V.-Division

(Dienstsiegel)

(Dienstgrad und Dienststellung)

SS-Gruppenführer und Div. Kommandeur

Iron Cross 1st class document, signed by divisional commander Paul Hausser, listing Weidinger's company command.

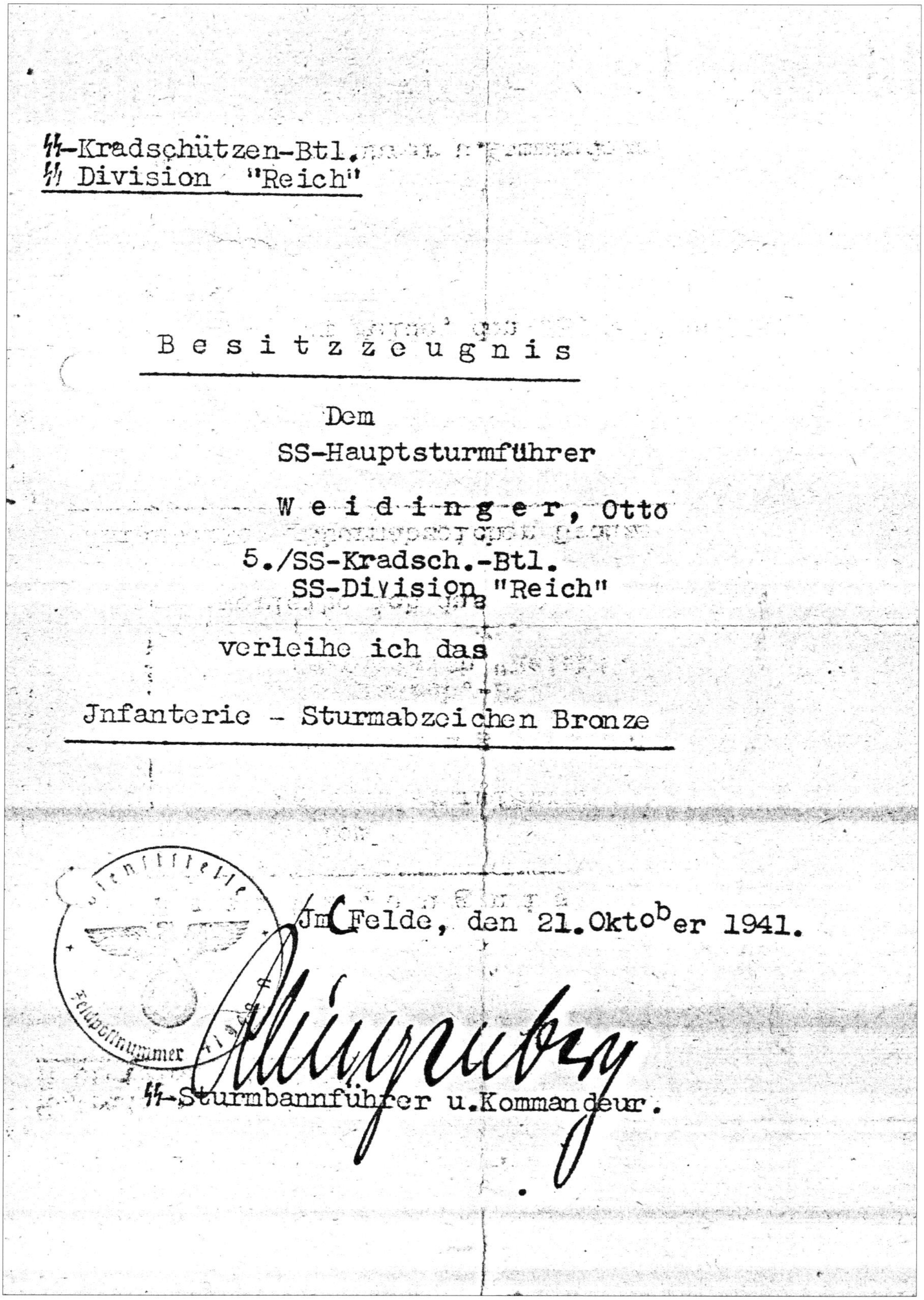

SS-Kradschützen-Btl.
SS Division "Reich"

B e s i t z z e u g n i s

Dem
SS-Hauptsturmführer
W e i d i n g e r, Otto
5./SS-Kradsch.-Btl.
SS-Division "Reich"

verleihe ich das

Jnfanterie – Sturmabzeichen Bronze

Jm Felde, den 21.Oktober 1941.

SS-Sturmbannführer u.Kommandeur.

Signed by Knight's Cross holder Fritz Klingenberg, the Infantry Assault Badge in Bronze document given to Weidinger in the field.

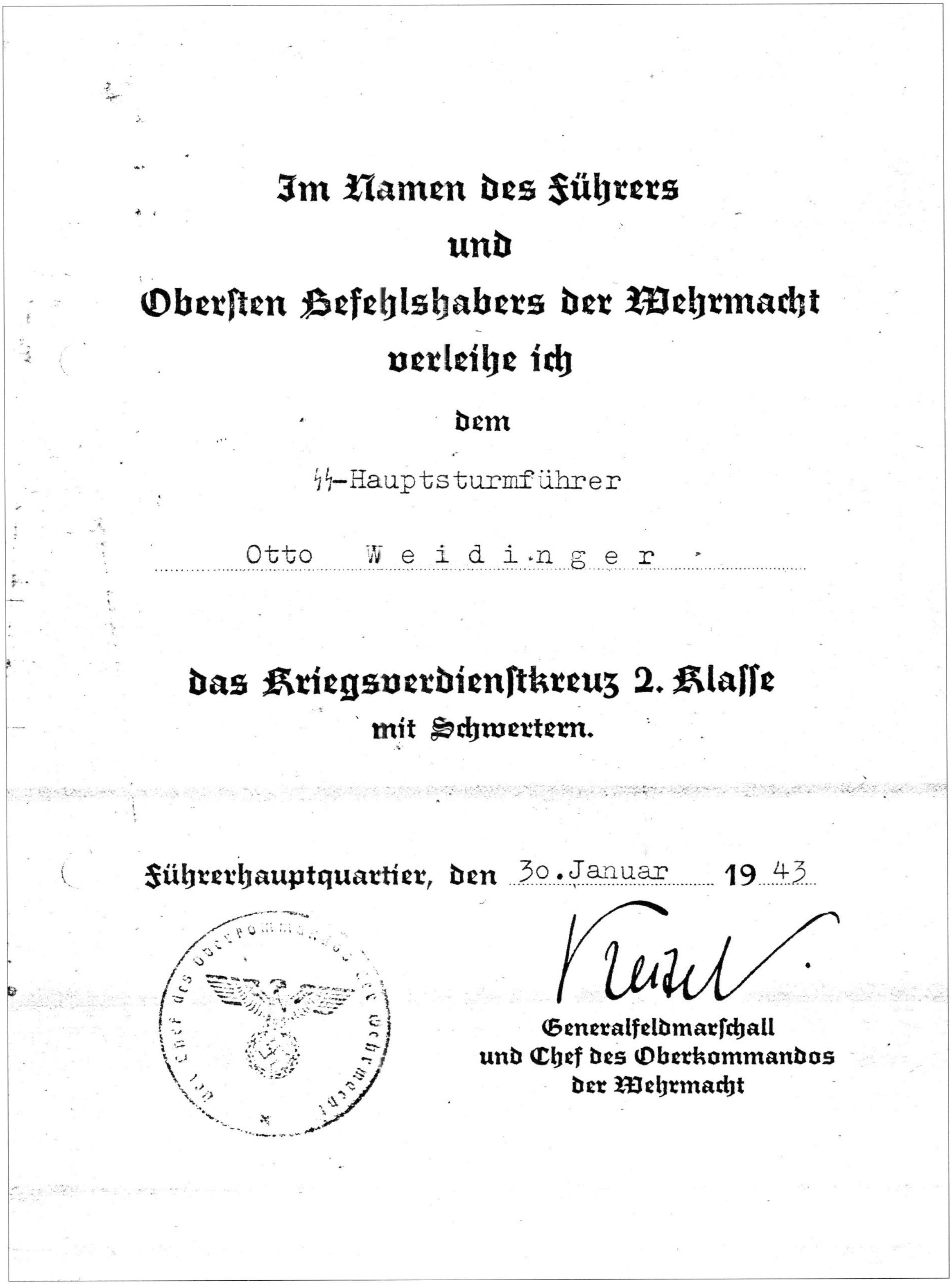

Im Namen des Führers

und

Obersten Befehlshabers der Wehrmacht

verleihe ich

dem

ᛋᛋ-Hauptsturmführer

Otto Weidinger

das Kriegsverdienstkreuz 2. Klasse

mit Schwertern.

Führerhauptquartier, den 30.Januar 1943

Keitel

Generalfeldmarschall

und Chef des Oberkommandos

der Wehrmacht

Showing a stamped Wilhelm Keitel signature, above is Weidinger's award certificate for the War Merit Cross 2nd class with Swords.

2. SS-Pz.Div."Das Reich" Div.St.Qu., 3.4.44

Reichsführer-SS Persönl. Stab
Verb. Offz. b. OKH / PA / P 5
Eingang 12. April 1944
Tgb. Nr. 367/44

Nr. 2994

V o r s c h l a g s l i s t e Nr. 3 3

für die

Verleihung des Ritterkreuzes des Eisernen Kreuzes

SS-Oberführer und Div.Kommandeur

An
SS-Sturmbannführer K m e n t
Verb.Offz.b.OKH/PA/P5 1.Staffel

Verliehen: 21.4.44

Cover page of the Knight's Cross recommendation for Otto Weidinger submitted by Heinz Lammerding. The approval at the bottom is the official award date.

VORLÄUFIGES BESITZZEUGNIS

DER FÜHRER

HAT DEM

SS-Sturmbannführer Weidinger
Kommandeur SS-Pz.Gren. Rgt."Das Reich"

DAS RITTERKREUZ

DES EISERNEN KREUZES

AM 21. 4.1944 VERLIEHEN

HQu OKH, DEN 24. April 1944

OBERKOMMANDO DES HEERES

I.A.

Burgdorf

GENERALLEUTNANT

Preliminary award certificate for the Knight's Cross with Wilhelm Burgdorf stamped signature. It lists Weidinger's then current posting while the recommendation itself was for 1943 combats leading the reconnaissance detachment.

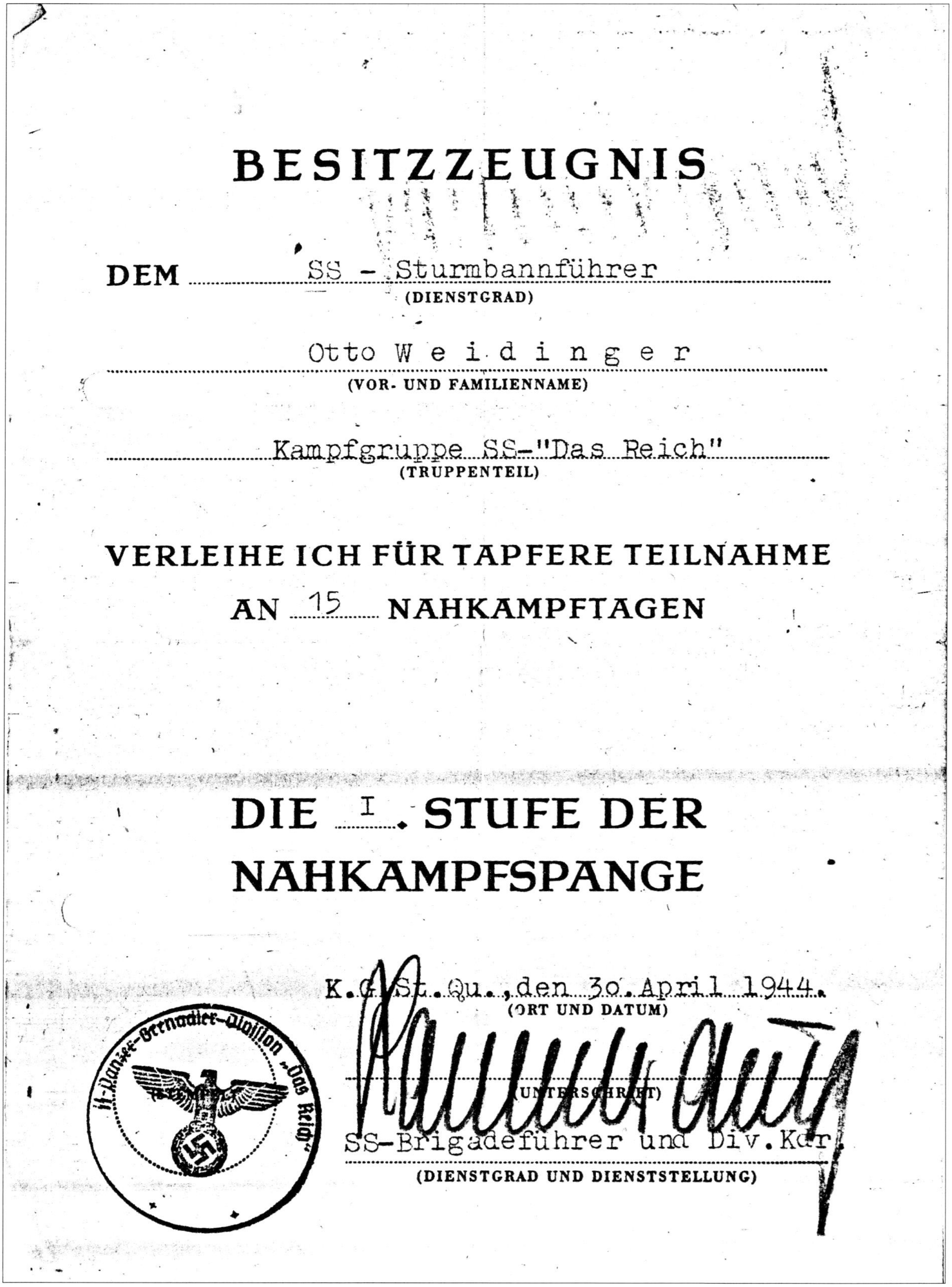
BESITZZEUGNIS

DEM SS - Sturmbannführer
(DIENSTGRAD)

Otto Weidinger
(VOR- UND FAMILIENNAME)

Kampfgruppe SS-"Das Reich"
(TRUPPENTEIL)

VERLEIHE ICH FÜR TAPFERE TEILNAHME
AN 15 NAHKAMPFTAGEN

DIE I. STUFE DER
NAHKAMPFSPANGE

K.G.St.Qu., den 30. April 1944.
(ORT UND DATUM)

(UNTERSCHRIFT)

SS-Brigadeführer und Div.Kdr.
(DIENSTGRAD UND DIENSTSTELLUNG)

The Close Combat Clasp in Bronze document signed by Heinz Lammerding.

Der Reichsführer-SS Feld-Kommandostelle, den 7.11.1944

An den
SS-Sturmbannführer der Waffen-SS

Otto W e i d i n g e r
SS-Nr. 114 921

Ich befördere Sie mit Wirkung vom 9. November 1944
zum SS-Obersturmbannführer der Waffen-SS.

Der Reichsführer-SS M/ [initials]

Signed by Heinrich Himmler, the document shown is for advancement to SS-Obersturmbannführer. All promotions from Sturmbannführer to Oberst-Gruppenführer were personally signed by Himmler (for field grade officers) or Hitler (General officers).

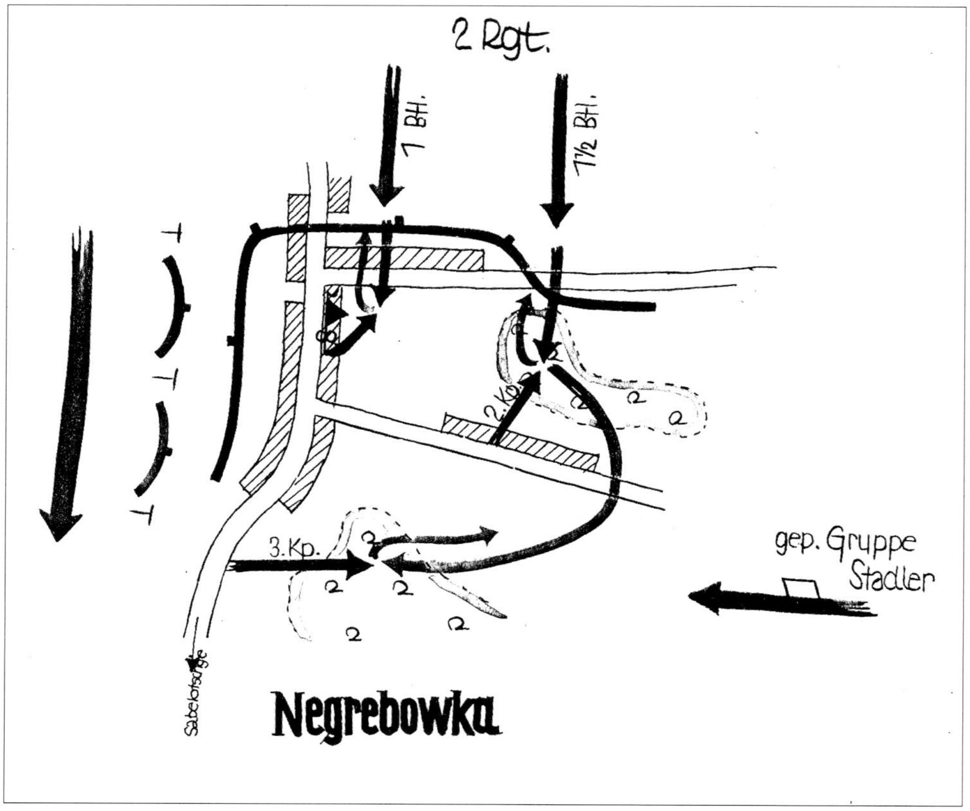

Situation maps attached to the recommendations for Otto Weidinger's Knight's Cross (above) and Oakleaves.

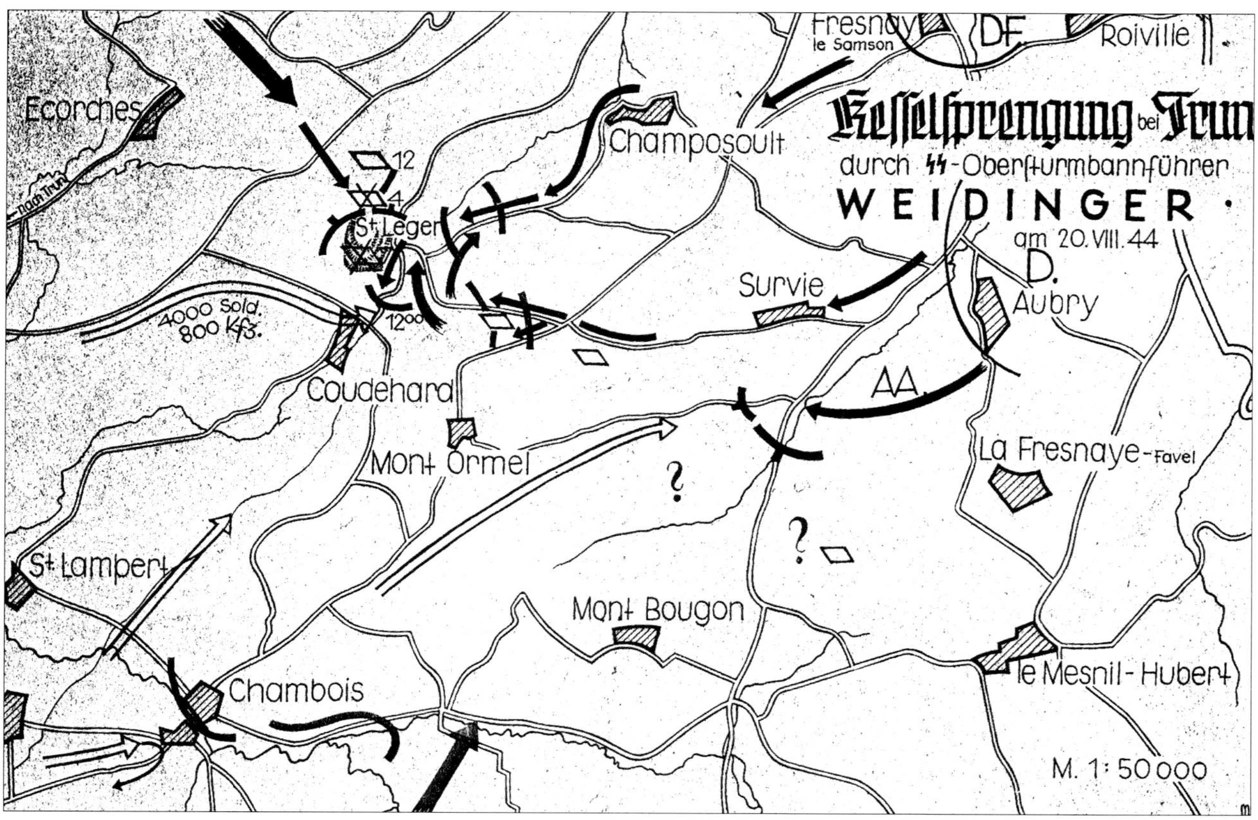

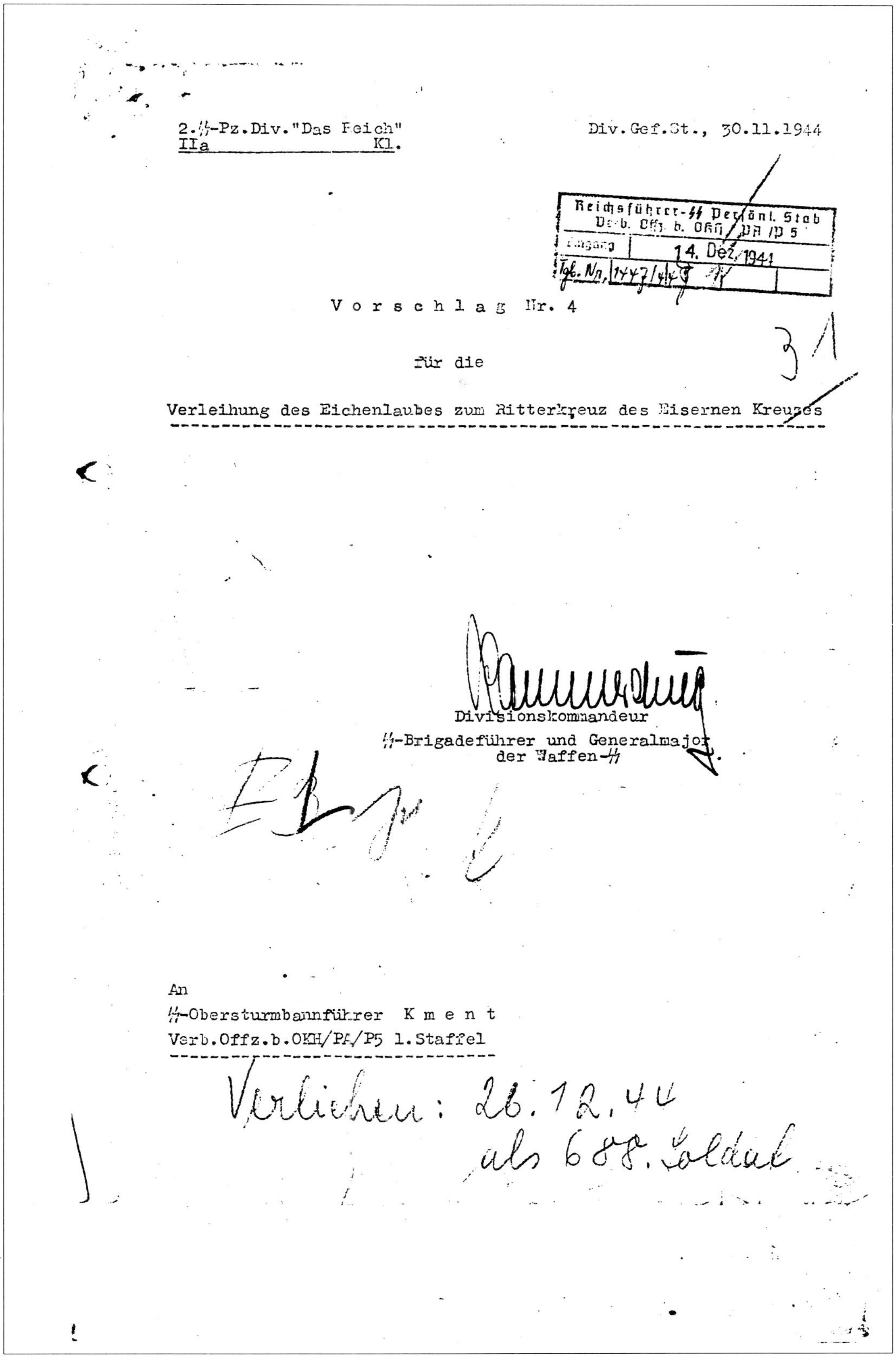

2.SS-Pz.Div."Das Reich" Div.Gef.St., 30.11.1944
IIa Kl.

Reichsführer-SS Persönl. Stab
Verb. Offz. b. OKH / PA / P 5
Eingang 14. Dez. 1944
Tgb. Nr. 1447/44

V o r s c h l a g Nr. 4

für die

Verleihung des Eichenlaubes zum Ritterkreuz des Eisernen Kreuzes

Divisionskommandeur
SS-Brigadeführer und Generalmajor
der Waffen-SS

An
SS-Obersturmbannführer K m e n t
Verb.Offz.b.OKH/PA/P5 1.Staffel

Verliehen: 26.12.44
als 688. Soldat

Recommendation document cover submitted by Heinz Lammerding for the award of the Oakleaves to Otto Weidinger. The approval as the 688th award is seen at the bottom.

Der Chef des Generalstabes
des Heeres

HQu., den 12.1.1945

Herrn
SS-Obersturmbannführer Weidinger
Kdr.SS-Pz.Gren.Rgt.4

Zu der hohen Auszeichnung, die Ihnen vom Führer am 26.12.44 verliehen worden ist, spreche ich Ihnen und Ihrem tapferen Regiment meine aufrichtigsten Glückwünsche aus.

Heil Hitler !

Guderian

A congratulatory note sent to Otto Weidinger by Panzer General Heinz Guderian after the award of the Oakleaves. Weidinger received numerous similar letters from senior civil and military officials.